Reach
HIGHER

Program Authors

Nancy Frey

Lada Kratky

Nonie K. Lesaux

Sylvia Linan-Thompson

Deborah J. Short

Jennifer D. Turner

NATIONAL GEOGRAPHIC

L E A R N I N G

Australia · Brazil · Mexico · Singapore · United Kingdom · United States

National Geographic Learning,
a Cengage Company

Reach Higher 5A
Program Authors: Nancy Frey, Lada Kratky,
Nonie K. Lesaux, Sylvia Linan-Thompson,
Deborah J. Short, Jennifer D. Turner

Publisher, Content-based English:
Erik Gundersen

Associate Director, R&D: Barnaby Pelter

Senior Development Editors:
Jacqueline Eu

Ranjini Fonseka

Kelsey Zhang

Director of Global Marketing: Ian Martin

Heads of Regional Marketing:
Charlotte Ellis (Europe, Middle East and Africa)

Kiel Hamm (Asia)

Irina Pereyra (Latin America)

Product Marketing Manager: David Spain

Senior Production Controller: Tan Jin Hock

Senior Media Researcher (Covers): Leila Hishmeh

Senior Designer: Lisa Trager

Director, Operations: Jason Seigel

Operations Support:
Rebecca Barbush

Drew Robertson

Caroline Stephenson

Nicholas Yeaton

Manufacturing Planner: Mary Beth Hennebury

Publishing Consultancy and Composition:
MPS North America LLC

For permission to use material from this text or product,
submit all requests online at **cengage.com/permissions**
Further permissions questions can be emailed to
permissionrequest@cengage.com

ISBN-13: 978-0-357-36699-8

National Geographic Learning
200 Pier Four Blvd
Boston, MA 02210
USA

Locate your local office at **international.cengage.com/region**

Visit National Geographic Learning online at **ELTNGL.com**
Visit our corporate website at **www.cengage.com**

Printed in China
Print Number: 08 Print Year: 2023

Contents at a Glance

Table of Contents

Crossing Between Cultures | Unit 1

? BIG QUESTION

How can where you are change who you are?

SOCIAL STUDIES
▸ Immigration

Part 1

Part 2

Table of Contents

Catching the Light

Unit 2

? BIG QUESTION

What is the power of the sun?

SCIENCE
▸ Energy

Table of Contents

Nature's Webs

Unit 3

? BIG QUESTION

How are animals and plants dependent on one another?

SCIENCE
- Food Webs
- Ecosystems

Table of Contents

Justice

(?) BIG QUESTION

What is justice?

SOCIAL STUDIES

▸ History: Human Rights

Genres at a Glance

Unit 1

Crossing
Between Cultures

? BIG Question

How can where you are change who you are?

FRANKFURT, GERMANY
German students learning Chinese calligraphy with a Chinese exchange teacher

Unit at a Glance
▷ **Language Focus**: Ask For and Give Information; Ask and Answer Questions
▷ **Reading Strategy**: Preview and Predict; Monitor and Clarify
▷ **Topic**: Immigration

Share What You Know

Do It!

❶ **Think** of two places you know that are different.

❷ **List** the ways they are different.

❸ **Share** your lists with the class.

Hawaii	Alaska
warm weather	cold weather
beach	snow
swimsuit	winter coat

Language Frames

- Where _____ ?
- I am from _____ .
- Now I live in _____ .

Ask For and Give Information

Listen to Lulu and Ricky's song. Then use **Language Frames** to ask for and give information about places you and your friends have lived.

Where Are You From?

Song

 Where does your family come from?
Can you explain to me?

 I am from a sunny island in the Caribbean Sea.
We lived in Puerto Rico till I was eight years old.
Now I live in Texas, where winters can be cold.
Where does your family come from?
I'd really like to know.

 I grew up in Indonesia, where I never saw the snow.
We lived close to the ocean, and swam all winter long.
Now I live in Texas, where I feel I belong.

Tune: "Yellow Rose of Texas"

Social Studies Vocabulary

Key Words

country

culture

education

employment

immigration

🔊 Key Words

Look at the photographs. Use **Key Words** and other words to talk about moving to a new **country**.

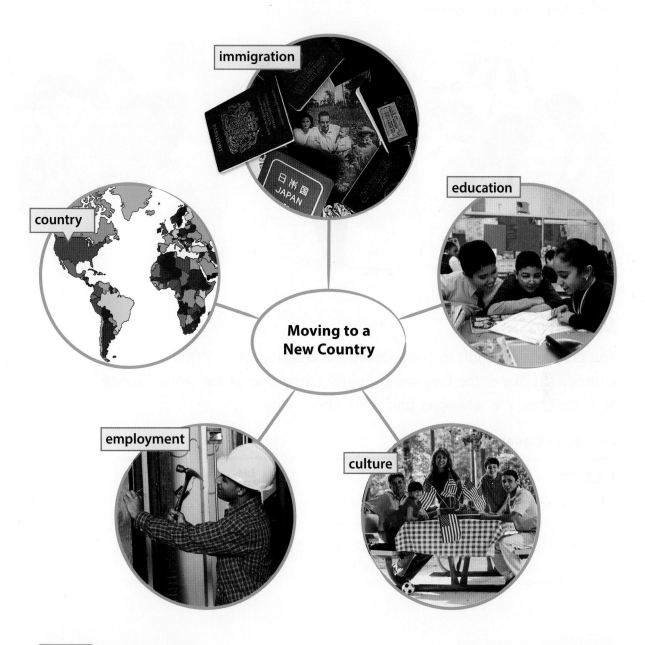

immigration

country

education

Moving to a New Country

employment

culture

Talk **Together**

How can moving to a new place change your life? With a partner, try to use **Language Frames** from page 4 and **Key Words** to ask for and give information.

Character Development

Story characters grow and change, just like you. When you understand **character development**, or how a character changes, you can understand the story better.

Map and Talk

You can make a chart to show character development. Write what the character is like at the beginning, middle, and end of the story. Notice how the character changes and think about why.

Character Development Chart

Beginning	Middle	End
Lulu is with her big family. She enjoys the warm weather and the beach.	Lulu misses her big family. She feels lonely. Cold weather is strange to her.	Lulu meets a friend and feels less lonely. She enjoys school.

Talk Together

Talk with a partner about a story in which the character changed. Explain how the character changed and why. Have your partner make a character development chart.

More Key Words

Use these words to talk about "My Diary Across Places and Time" and "I Was Dreaming to Come to America."

opportunity
noun

An **opportunity** is a good chance to do something. There is a job **opportunity** here.

refuge
noun

A **refuge** is a place where people go to be safe or to find shelter.

symbol
noun

A **symbol** is something that stands for something else. A heart shape is a **symbol** for love.

transition
noun

A **transition** is a change from one situation to another. Moving to a new city is a big **transition**.

translate
verb

When you **translate**, you change words and ideas from one language to another.

Talk Together

Use a **Key Word** to ask a question. Your partner answers using another **Key Word**.

> When do you have an opportunity to use two languages?

> When I translate English words into Spanish.

Learn to Preview and Predict

Look at the cartoon. The text does not say why Lulu and Ricky are at the store, but you can look for details in the picture. This is how you **preview**. Then you can make a guess about, or **predict**, what will happen next.

When you get ready to read, you **preview** and **predict**, too.

How to Preview and Predict

👁	**1.** Read the title. Look at the pictures.	I read _____. I see _____.
☁	**2.** Begin to read. Stop and make predictions.	I predict _____.
📖	**3.** Read on to check whether your predictions are correct or incorrect. Confirm your prediction or make a new one.	My prediction _____.

Talk Together

Read Lulu's blog entries. Read the sample prediction. Then use **Language Frames** to tell a partner about your prediction.

Blog

LULU'S Blog

https://eltngl.com/reachhigherseries

Lulu's Blog

HOME | ABOUT THIS BLOG | PICTURES

April 5 | **Author:** Lulu

Today a new student came to our class. She is from Puerto Rico, too! :) Ms. Keller made me her buddy. She said I could **translate** for her until she learned more English. This is a great **opportunity** for me to help Ana feel comfortable. I know how scared I felt when I started school! I want Ana's **transition** to American **culture** to be easier.

April 20 | **Author:** Lulu

As usual, Ricky, Ana, and I sat together at lunch. We had fun planning my birthday party. Ana understands why I miss my family so much. She says she has a special surprise for me that will make us both less homesick for Puerto Rico. ◀

May 10 | **Author:** Lulu

My party was so fun! I could not believe that Ana asked her cousins to come and play Puerto Rican music at the party. Since we had *arroz con gandules y pernil* (rice and beans with meat), too, I really felt like our home was a **refuge** today for all of us who miss Puerto Rico. Still, I love the United States. I wore red, white, and blue as a **symbol** of my happiness here. Now I am looking forward to our next party on the Fourth of July! ◀

"I read that a new girl has moved from Puerto Rico.

I *see* a smiley face in Lulu's diary entry.

I predict that Lulu and Ana will become good friends.

My prediction was correct!"

◀ = A good place to make a prediction

Read a Story

Genre

A **diary** is a record of a person's thoughts, feelings, and experiences. This story is a fictional diary. It is a record of a character's thoughts, feelings, and experiences.

Narrator

In fiction, the narrator is the person who tells the story. The narrator can be a character in the story, or just a voice describing the events. In "My Diary Across Places and Time," the narrator is a character named Aberto, who tells the story by writing in his diary.

Dear Diary,

I can't sleep! Thank you for being here for me when I have so much to tell you. Tonight, after my sisters and I climbed into our beds, I overheard whispers between Mom and Dad.

My Diary Across Places and Time

by Robyn Montana Turner

▶ Set a Purpose
Aberto discovers that his
family is moving. Find out why.

Dear Diary,

I can't sleep! Thank you for being here for me when I have so much to tell you. Tonight, after my sisters and I climbed into our beds, I overheard **whispers** between Mom and Dad. They said we are going to leave our home in New Jersey to **move** back to Brazil. Five years is a long time to live in this place I have come to know as home. Will I ever see it again?

whispers soft words
move go to a different place to live

Mom **broke the news** at breakfast after Dad left for work.
"You know how much your father loves his job," she said. "He
was a great soccer player, and then he worked hard to become
a coach, organizing soccer camps for children in this **country** .
Now he wants to move his soccer camps to Brazil, our **homeland**."
Then Mom added, "Your grandparents are growing
old, as well. Try to understand."

Why didn't my sisters feel sad, like I did?

broke the news told us
homeland the **country**
you were born in

My best friend, Hugo, and I met **on the field** after school today. We promised never to forget each other. I've known Hugo since the first day we arrived in New Jersey, when I was only five. Will I ever find a friend like him in Brazil?

"At least your dad has his own business plan," said Hugo. "Right now, my dad has no **employment**."

on the field where the teams play soccer

15

Soon, we will **pack our van** and leave for Brazil. Dad will drive the soccer camp bus, filled with our boxes. I'll probably ride with him, and Mom will drive the van with my sisters. I can't believe they still don't seem to be upset about leaving the only home they've ever known. By now, both Mom and Dad are **excited** about the move. It looks like I'm the only one who isn't okay with this big **transition**.

What if I can't remember how to speak Portuguese in Brazil? And now I have a new worry—where will I go to school? I had hoped to get my **education** with Hugo here in New Jersey!

While we were packing boxes, Dad **patted my shoulder**. "Aberto, I can see how worried you've been. Everything will be all right. You like to play soccer, and you want to go to a good school, don't you? We will work to make it all happen for you."

Blankets

Photos

Books

pack our van put our things in the vehicle
excited very happy
patted my shoulder touched my shoulder gently

▶ **Before You Continue**

1. **Explain** Why is Aberto moving to a new **country**?
2. **Character** How does Aberto feel about leaving his home? Find evidence in the text to support your answer.

▶ **Predict**
What will happen on the
first part of the journey?

Our trip was long and hard. **Tumbleweeds** gathered along roadsides in West Texas, and the nights grew cold, so we huddled together as we slept in the van. When we crossed the border into Mexico, Dad presented our passports to the officials. I peeked out the bus window to see large buildings made of carved stone, smelled breakfast tacos cooking, and heard children playing in the plaza. Was I too tired from the traveling, or was I already accepting the idea of a whole new **culture**?

Tumbleweeds large balls formed by dried out plants

From Mexico, we traveled through Central America—each **country** had its own entry requirements, sights, smells, and sounds—until we reached South America. One afternoon, as Dad drove along, he grew quiet for a while and then talked to me like I was a grown man. "Aberto," he said **pensively**, "when we get to Brazil, we will have **challenges** ahead. I am going to need your help." Then Dad explained how I fit into his business plan.

pensively thinking deeply
challenges difficulties

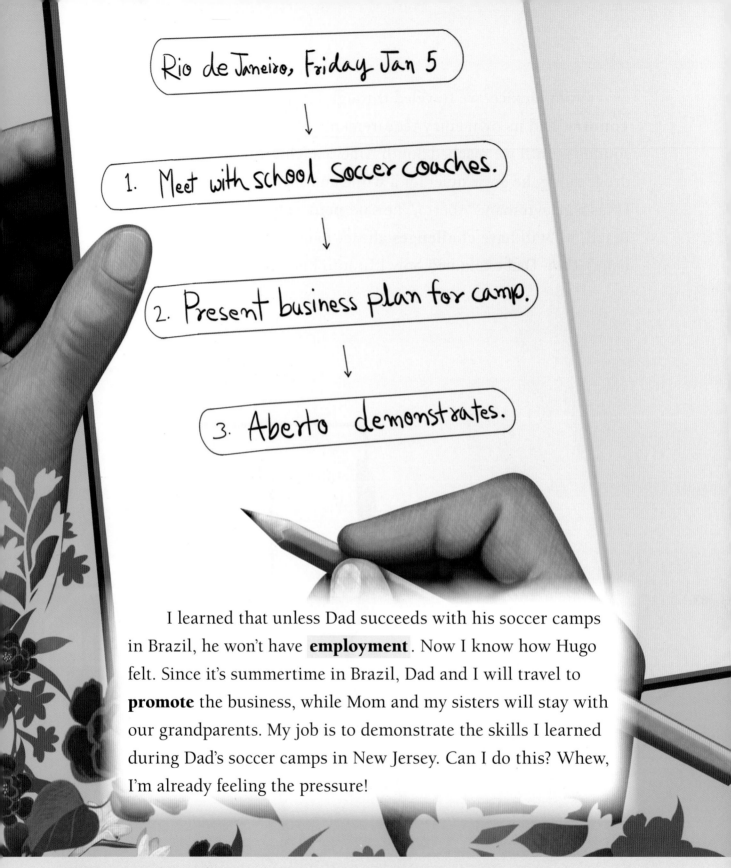

Rio de Janeiro, Friday Jan 5

↓

1. Meet with school soccer coaches.

↓

2. Present business plan for camp.

↓

3. Aberto demonstrates.

I learned that unless Dad succeeds with his soccer camps in Brazil, he won't have **employment**. Now I know how Hugo felt. Since it's summertime in Brazil, Dad and I will travel to **promote** the business, while Mom and my sisters will stay with our grandparents. My job is to demonstrate the skills I learned during Dad's soccer camps in New Jersey. Can I do this? Whew, I'm already feeling the pressure!

promote present their work to other people

By the time our van and bus reached Brazil, I had written down my part in Dad's business plan. We talked and, as we drove, I told my dad that I was nervous about **pitching** in a language I was not familiar with. Dad told me not to worry about it, and we **envisioned** how each meeting with soccer coaches would **roll out**. Dad and I took turns practicing our pitch to the coaches and planning which skills I'd showcase. By evening, we were polished professionals. But will the plan work in a **culture** I can **barely** remember? We'll find out soon. First stop: My birthplace, Rio de Janeiro.

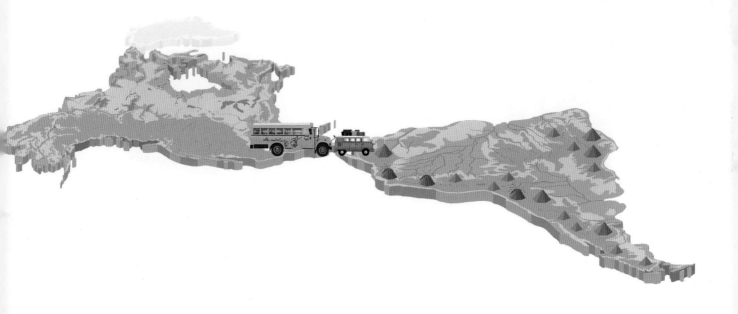

pitching attempting to persuade
envisioned imagined
roll out happen
barely not remember very well

▶ **Before You Continue**

1. **Character** What happens on the first part of the journey? How does this make Aberto feel?

2. **Clarify** Why was Aberto's father interested in succeeding in Brazil?

Grandma and Grandpa greeted us with open arms and big hugs. A warm pot of *moqueca* loaded with fresh fish, rice, and coconut milk, like Mom used to cook in New Jersey, just **hit the spot**. The next morning, Dad and I set out to contact coaches in the area. By late afternoon, we had three invitations to meet with teams next week, where my part of the business plan will kick in. Suddenly I'm terrified—and excited.

◀ *moqueca* a Brazilian dish
hit the spot felt good

We stayed with Grandma and Grandpa until we found our own place to live.

Mom and my sisters seemed to be very happy about the new house, but I was still thinking about what we left behind. This wasn't home to me. Dad and I talked about how I felt and he hugged me and said, "Son, in a few weeks, this will feel like home."

Well, Diary, I finally found a place where I can sit, think, and write. It may not be my bed in New Jersey, but it's more comfy than the pad in the bus. You know, I may be far away from my good friend Hugo, but he's in my memory through these words on your pages. He gave me a blue cap as a farewell present and for good wishes for my new life. And Diary, I think it's working. ❖

▶ **Before You Continue**

1. **Character** How does Aberto feel about where he lives now?
2. **Draw Conclusions** Why are Aberto's blue cap and diary important to him?

Meet the Author
Robyn Montana Turner

AWARD WINNER

Robyn Montana Turner likes to write stories and books for children. In her career, she has written 25 books, many of them focusing on art and artists. Just as Aberto in this story grew to enjoy keeping a journal about his travels to another country, so too does the author enjoy adventure and journaling. She has traveled extensively, taking notes in her journal, gaining inspiration for yet more stories and books. Currently she enjoys traveling to attend concerts of well-known musician, Paul McCartney, whose band, *The Beatles*, was a hit when Turner was a teenager.

◀ Author Robyn Montana Turner

Writer's Craft

The author includes details about how things look and feel to Aberto, including the smell of breakfast tacos and the cold at night. Imagine that you are Aberto. Write a new diary entry about your journey to Brazil. Include sensory details, such as how things look, smell, taste, sound, or feel.

PART 1 **Think and Respond**

Key Words	
country	opportunity
culture	refuge
education	symbol
employment	transition
immigration	translate

Talk About It

1. What do **diary entries** tell you about the character who wrote them? Use examples from Aberto's diary to explain your answer.

   Diary entries tell you what the character _____ .
   Aberto's diary entries tell readers what he _____ .

2. What **information** might Aberto give about himself to his new friends in Brazil?

3. How can Aberto keep the American **culture** alive as he makes the **transition** to life in Brazil?

Write About It

What exciting **opportunities** do you think Aberto and his family will find in Brazil? Write three sentences. Use **Key Words** to explain your ideas.

They will have an **opportunity** to _____ .

Character Development

Use a character development chart to show how Aberto changed during "My Diary Across Places and Time." Think about how Aberto feels as he makes the move to Brazil.

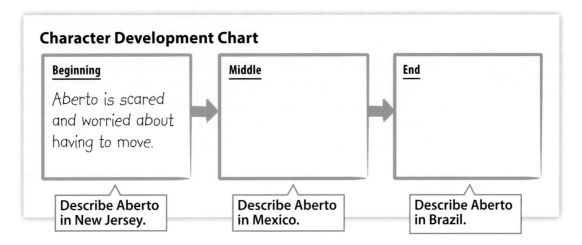

Character Development Chart

Beginning	Middle	End
Aberto is scared and worried about having to move.		

Describe Aberto in New Jersey.   Describe Aberto in Mexico.   Describe Aberto in Brazil.

Now use your character development chart as you retell the story to a partner. Be sure to explain how Aberto changes throughout the story. Use **Key Words** in your retelling.

> In the beginning of the story, Aberto _____ .
> In the middle of the story, Aberto _____ .
> By the end of the story, Aberto _____ .

Fluency

Practice reading with expression. Rate your reading.

Talk Together

How does the move change Aberto? Write a song or chant about Aberto's move. Include **Key Words**. Share your song or chant with the class.

Use a Dictionary

When you come to a word you don't know, use a **dictionary** to find the word's meaning and more information about it.

> These **symbols** show how to pronounce a word and how to break it into syllables.

> The word *promise* can be used as a **noun** and as a **verb**.

¹**promise** /ˈprɑːmˈɪs/ **noun** **1**: a statement that you will do something **2**: a reason for hope or success *Her work shows great promise.* **3**: something you say you will do [Middle English, from Latin *prōmissum*, past participle of *prōmittere* to send forth, to project, to promise, from *prō-* forth and *mittere* to send.]

²**promise** /ˈprɑːmɪs/ **verb** to say you will do something *I promise to write to you.*

Try It Together

Read the dictionary entry. Then answer the questions.

¹**country** /ˈkʌnˈtri/ **noun 1**: an area of land with its own government *Every country has its own flag.* **2**: a place that is not close to a city or town *He lives in the country.* [Middle English, from Old French *contree*, from Medieval Latin *contrāta* "lying opposite" (used of a land or region). Ultimately from Latin *contrā* facing, opposite.]

1. **How many meanings does the dictionary give for country?**

   A one

   B two

   C three

   D four

2. **How many syllables are there in country?**

   A one

   B two

   C three

   D four

I Was Dreaming to Come to America

written and illustrated by
Veronica Lawlor

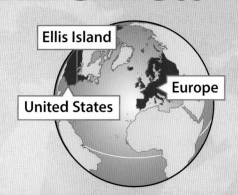

In the year 1900, most people who moved to the United States came from Europe. They traveled by ship across the Atlantic Ocean, in search of better lives. Many of these immigrants had to stop at Ellis Island, a tiny island near New York City, before they were allowed to officially enter the United States. For many of them, Ellis Island was a **symbol** of both a long journey and a new life.

Here, four immigrants describe their arrival at Ellis Island.

to Come of Coming

▶ **Before You Continue**
1. **Explain** Why was Ellis Island a **symbol** for immigrants from Europe?
2. **Predict** How do you think a variety of viewpoints will help you understand what it was like to arrive at Ellis Island?

"My first impressions of the new world
will always **remain etched** in my memory,
particularly that hazy October morning
when I first saw Ellis Island.

The **steamer** Florida,
14 days out of Naples,
filled to capacity with 1,600 natives of Italy,
had weathered one of the worst storms
in our captain's memory.

Glad we were, both children and grown-ups,
to leave the open sea
and come at last
through the narrows into the bay.

My mother, my stepfather, my brother Giuseppe,
and my two sisters, Liberta and Helvetia,
all of us together,
happy that we had come through the storm safely,
clustered on the foredeck
for fear of separation
and looked with wonder
on this miraculous land of our dreams."

> Edward Corsi
> Italy
> Arrived in 1907 • Age 10

foredeck

remain etched stay
◀ **steamer** a type of ship
filled to capacity completely filled
clustered on the foredeck stood
together at the front of the ship

▶ **Before You Continue**

1. **Analyze** How do you know that the text on page 30 represents the words of Edward Corsi?

2. **Interpret** What does the picture show about Edward Corsi's journey to the U.S.?

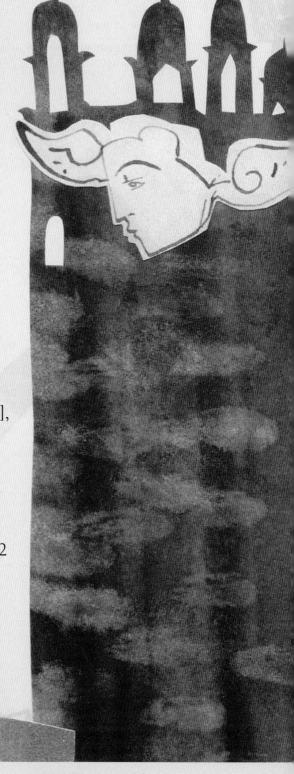

"I'd never seen such a big building [Ellis Island]—
the size of it. I think the size of it **got to me**.
According to the houses I left in my town,
this was like a whole city in one,
in one building.

It was an enormous thing to see, I tell you.
I almost felt smaller than I am
to see that beautiful [building],
it looked beautiful.

My basket, my little basket,
that's all I had with me.
There were hardly any things.

My mother gave me the *sorrah* [a kind of sandwich],
and I had one change of clothes.
That's what I brought from Europe."

Celia Adler
Russia
Arrived in 1914 • Age 12

got to me surprised me
According Compared
There were hardly any things.
   I did not have much in my
   basket.

ORAL HISTORY #3

"I feel like I had two lives.
You plant something in the ground,
it has its roots,
and then you **transplant** it
where it stays permanently.

That's what happened to me.
You put an end...
and forget about your childhood;
I became a man here.

All of a sudden, I started life new,
amongst people whose language
I didn't understand...

[It was a] different life;
everything was different...
but **I never despaired**,
I was optimistic.

And this is the only **country**
where you're not a stranger,
because we are all strangers.
It's **only a matter of time**
who got here first."

Lazarus Salamon
Hungary
Arrived in 1920 • Age 16

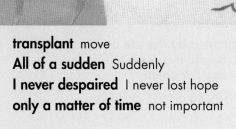

transplant move
All of a sudden Suddenly
I never despaired I never lost hope
only a matter of time not important

▶ **Before You Continue**

1. **Clarify** Why did Celia Adler feel so small when she got to Ellis Island?

2. **Figurative Language** What comparison does Lazarus Salamon make to help you understand his **transition**?

ORAL HISTORY #4

"The language was a problem of course,
but it was **overcome**
by the use of interpreters.
We had interpreters on the island
who spoke **practically** every language.

overcome by the use of interpreters
helped by people who
could **translate**
practically almost; nearly

It would happen sometimes
that these interpreters—some of them—
were really **softhearted** people
and hated to see people being **deported**,
and they would, at times,
help the **aliens** by interpreting
in such a manner
as to **benefit** the alien
and not the government.

Unless you saw it,
you couldn't visualize
the misery of these people
who came to the United States from Europe...

They were tired;
they had gone through
an awful lot of hardships.

It's impossible for anyone
who had not gone through the experience
to imagine what it was." ❖

Edward Ferro
Inspector, Ellis Island
Italy
Arrived in 1906 • Age 12

---

softhearted kind; caring
deported sent back to their **countries**
aliens people from other **countries**
benefit help

▶ **Before You Continue**

1. **Clarify** In what ways did the interpreters help the immigrants?
2. **Use Text Features** What is Edward Ferro's job? How do you know?

Respond and Extend

Key Words

country	opportunity
culture	refuge
education	symbol
employment	transition
immigration	translate

Compare Genres

Fiction and nonfiction are different forms of writing, or genres. How are the two genres the same? How are they different? Work with a partner to complete the Venn diagram.

Venn Diagram

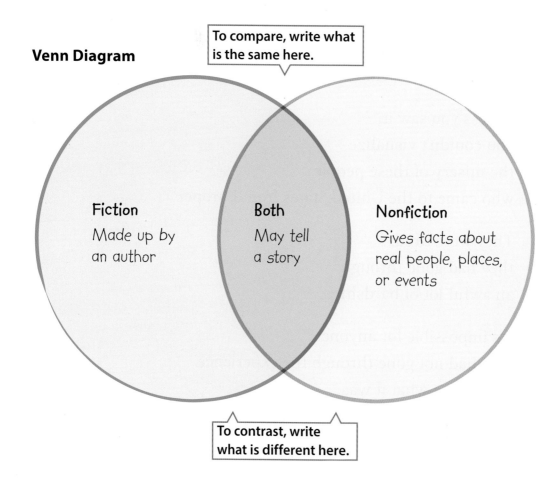

To compare, write what is the same here.

Fiction
Made up by an author

Both
May tell a story

Nonfiction
Gives facts about real people, places, or events

To contrast, write what is different here.

Talk Together

Can where you are change who you are? Think about Aberto's diary and Lulu's blog about **immigration**. Use **Key Words** to talk about your ideas.

Complete Sentences

A sentence tells a complete thought. A sentence starts with a capital letter and has an end mark. A **complete sentence** has two main parts.

| Our little house in New Jersey | seems so far away. |

subject : what or whom the sentence is about

predicate : what the subject is, does, or has

Grammar Rules   Parts of a Complete Sentence

The **complete subject** includes all the words that tell about the subject. The **simple subject** is the most important noun.	**My friend** Juanita arrived in America a month ago.
The **complete predicate** includes the verb and all the other words in the predicate. The **simple predicate** is the verb.	My friend Juanita **arrived** **in** **America a month ago**.

Read Complete Sentences

Read the sentences below from "My Diary Across Places and Time." What is the complete subject and predicate in each sentence?

We promised never to forget each other.
Grandma and Grandpa greeted us with open arms and big hugs.

Write Complete Sentences

Write a sentence about one of the pictures in "I Was Dreaming to Come to America." Be sure that the sentence has a complete subject and complete predicate. Read your sentence aloud and compare it with a partner's.

Language Frames

• Can you _____ ?
• Yes, I can. I _____ .
• Do you like _____ ?
• Yes I do. I _____ .

Ask and Answer Questions

Listen to the dialogue between Joe and Grandpa Joseph. Then use **Language Frames** to ask and answer questions.

Dialogue

Memories

Joe: Grandpa, can you remember your farm in Hungary?

Grandpa: Yes, I can. I was your age when we left.

Joe: Was it fun to live on a farm?

Grandpa: Yes, it was. But I like big cities, too.

Joe: Do you like New York?

Grandpa: Yes, I do. I love New York!

🔊 Key Words

Look at the photographs. Use **Key Words** and other words to talk about people's **customs** and their countries of **origin** .

Key Words

citizenship

custom

ethnic

foreign

origin

▲ Every day in the United States, immigrants arrive from **foreign** countries.

Many take the oath of **citizenship** to become American citizens. ▷

◁ **Ethnic** foods, such as pizza, falafel, and spring rolls, were brought to the United States by immigrants.

Talk Together

Do you have to change who you are to fit in? Why? Use **Language Frames** from page 38 and **Key Words** to ask and answer this question with a partner.

Compare and Contrast

When you **compare and contrast**, you think about how two things are alike and how they are different.

▲ Joseph on Farm   ▲ Joseph in City

Map and Talk

You can use a Venn diagram to show how two things are alike and different.

Venn Diagram

To compare, write what is the same here.

Joseph on Farm	Both	Joseph in City
born on farm	have good and bad times	moved to New York at age 10
farm life	have family and friends	city life
world war		learns new language and customs

To contrast, write what is different here.

Talk **Together**

Talk with your partner about a day at school and a day at home.
Create a Venn diagram to compare and contrast these two days.

More Key Words

Use these words to talk about "A Writer's Journey" and "Migrant Stories from Around the World."

adapt
verb

If you **adapt,** you change. Visitors to Japan must **adapt** to a new way of eating.

challenge
noun

A **challenge** is a difficult task or situation. Carrying all the books at once is a **challenge**.

diversity
noun

The **diversity** of a group is how different the members of the group are.

identity
noun

Your **identity** makes you who you are. Playing music is part of this boy's **identity**.

society
noun

A **society** is a group of people who share rules and customs. Our **society** has safety rules.

Talk Together

Work with a partner. Make a Word Web of examples for each **Key Word**.

new school   new home

adapt to

new friends   new foods

41

Learn to Monitor and Clarify

Look at the movie poster. The picture does not tell you what the movie is about. But you can ask yourself a question about what you see. This is how you **monitor** your understanding. Then you can read more closely to find the answer, or to **clarify** your understanding.

When you read, you can **monitor** and **clarify**, too.

How to Monitor and Clarify

	1. When you do not understand the text, stop. Think about what the text means.	What does _____ mean?
	2. If you do not understand, reread the text. If the meaning is still not clear, read on.	I will _____.
	3. Think about how the meaning has become clearer to you.	It means _____.

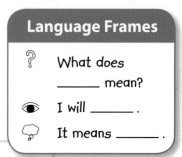

Talk Together

Read the rest of Grandpa Joseph and Joe's discussion. Look at the sample. Then use **Language Frames** to tell a partner about how you monitor your reading.

Interview

Grandpa Joseph's Move

Joe: It must have been a really big **challenge** for you to **adapt** to your new home in the United States.

Grandpa Joseph: It was very different here! In Hungary, almost everyone was the same. Here, people came from many countries. There was greater **ethnic diversity** than in Hungary. In our neighborhood, everyone was from someplace else.

Joe: Did you have to change to fit in?

Grandpa Joseph: We came from Hungary. My family did not want to forget our **origins**, so we kept some Hungarian **customs**. We still spoke our language at home, and Mama cooked the same foods. But we also added some American customs to our lives.

Joe: So you became a Hungarian-American?

Grandpa Joseph: That's right! I became part of a new **society**. I got my American **citizenship** in 1965. I had a new **identity**. I was now a Hungarian-American.

Joe: That's what I am, too!

"What does ethnic diversity mean?

I will read on to find out.

It means people from many countries."

◄ = A good place to monitor and clarify your reading

43

Read a Biography

Genre

A **biography** is the story of a person's life. It is about important events that happen to that person and is written by someone else.

Point of View

Point of view describes how a story is told. In this biography, the narrator tells us about a person's thoughts and feelings. Sometimes this can make us feel like we are living in the story, too!

Xiaolu prepared to travel to England. She imagined that she would smell the breezes brought by the Atlantic Ocean and walk through gentle rains.

Her mother was worried. "They don't know how to cook rice in the West!" she said. "What will you eat?"

A Writer's Journey

A biography of Xiaolu Guo
by Penelope McKimm

▶ **Set a Purpose**
Find out how Xiaolu Guo's life
changed when she moved from
China to England.

*W*hen Xiaolu Guo was a child, she lived with her grandparents in Shitang, a fishing village in the southeastern region of China. Her grandfather was a fisherman, like most of the other men in the village. The family did not have a lot of money, and sometimes her grandfather sold objects that he found **washed up** on the beach to make some extra money.

Xiaolu was close to her grandmother, who looked after her. Her grandparents had never been to school, and for the first few years of Xiaolu's life, there were no books and no television in her home. She did not learn to read until she was eight years old.

washed up left by the sea

▲ Xiaolu Guo grew up in Shitang, a fishing village in southeast China

Shitang is in the far southeast of China, and it is famous for being the first place in the country to see **sunrise**. To celebrate this, the Chinese government built a monument in the year 2000. The monument faces out to sea and reflects the light of the sun as it comes over the horizon. Later, a museum of astronomy was built near the monument.

The fishermen of Shitang once had many **superstitions**. They used to paint eyes on their boats to make them look like dragons. They believed that this would make their boats more powerful and better able to survive the journeys at sea. Although they lived by the sea and made their living from it, the fishermen never learned to swim because they were afraid that they would be taken by monsters if they went in the water.

sunrise the moment when the sun appears
superstitions beliefs

There was a bus station in the village, and Xiaolu liked to talk to the stationmaster. She **admired** him because he had been to many places and knew many things. The stationmaster told her stories about old China and her ancestors, and about the people who had once come to the village from islands across the sea. He told her stories of pirates and warriors. Her favorite stories were about heroes who traveled to distant places and had adventures.

Xiaolu **longed to** explore the world one day to see **foreign** countries. As she grew older, she began to read about the countries of **the West**. She read books by authors from England and France and wondered what these places were like.

admired wanted to be like

longed to wanted very much to

the West North America, Central America, South America, Western Europe, and Great Britain

▲ **Xiaolu travels from Beijing to London.**

Xiaolu grew older and began to write books and make films. When she was in her **late twenties**, she applied for a scholarship to study in England. More than 500 people applied for the scholarship. One day, Xiaolu received a phone call from Beijing.

"Congratulations! You have won a scholarship!" she was told. The scholarship would pay for her to study at the National Film and Television School in England.

Xiaolu prepared to travel to England. She imagined that she would smell the breezes brought by the Atlantic Ocean and walk through gentle rains.

Her mother was worried. "They don't know how to cook rice in the West!" she said. "What will you eat?"

late twenties between 26 and 29 years old

▶ **Before You Continue**

1. **Clarify** How did Xiaolu become interested in traveling?
2. **Describe** What was Xiaolu's village like? How do we know this?

Xiaolu and her family were very excited. They had never visited the West, but they had seen films and television shows about England. The characters were rich and **well dressed**, and they lived in beautiful, big houses. The children went to **prestigious** boarding schools. Xiaolu loved to read books by English and other European writers, and she believed that the West was a good place for great writers. Xiaolu dreamed that one day, people in the West might read her books, too.

When Xiaolu arrived in England, it was raining. But instead of the gentle rain she had imagined, it was hard and cold. Instead of the sea breeze she had imagined, there were funny smells. Instead of beautiful, big houses, she saw short, gray buildings against the dark sky. She saw people who were not well dressed, and she didn't see any rich people.

well dressed wore nice clothes
prestigious very famous and respected

It took Xiaolu many months to **settle into** life in England.
She did not know anyone, and for a while she was very lonely
and **homesick**. It was expensive to commute, to buy food, and
to pay the bills, so after all those expenses, there was not a lot
of money left. There were many things about the English culture
that she did not understand, and she made many mistakes. She
saw that England was very different from the films and television
shows she had seen in China. Just like every other country,
England had its problems, too.

settle into get used to
homesick missing home

But her biggest **challenge** was the language. English was difficult, and this made it hard for her to participate in her classes or to make friends. With only a little English, she felt **isolated** from other people. She loved to read and write, but when she tried to do it in English, she would quickly become tired and frustrated. When she tried to give opinions in class, she could not find the right words.

The filmmaking classes at the National Film and Television School were very different from what she had experienced in China. Sometimes, her classmates laughed at her and called her ideas **old-fashioned**, and Xiaolu felt angry and hurt.

isolated separated
old-fashioned not modern

Xiaolu started visiting a local tea shop near the National Film and Television School. When she was not taking classes, she would sit in the tea shop for hours and read her English dictionary. Trying to save money, she would order only a cup of hot water to make tea, but then she realized that in England, this didn't show **good manners**. She learned that if she was a good customer, the owners would not mind her sitting in the tea shop for hours as she studied her English books.

The town where Xiaolu went to school was very small, and everyone who went to the tea shop seemed to know one another. They began to talk to Xiaolu, asking her how she was and whether she missed her family.

good manners politeness

Xiaolu lived in a village near the National Film and Television School so that she could save money on the commute. But she did not really like the village. There was not much for her to do except sit in the tea shop with her dictionary. The people living in the village were kind, but she did not have real friends there.

Finally, Xiaolu decided to move to London. At first, she was worried about being farther away from the National Film and Television School. However, she soon began to feel happier. There were more things to see and do, and she now lived closer to some of her classmates. She explored the city and took photographs of the Houses of Parliament and other famous **sights** in London.

sights interesting places

London is a city where people speak many different languages, and more than **one-third** of the people living there were not born in England. People come to London from all over the world. After moving there, Xiaolu met other people from China, as well as people from India, Pakistan, the Caribbean, and many other parts of the world.

Xiaolu discovered that she enjoyed the **diversity** of the big city. She **was surrounded by** people from all over the world, and, like her, many of them were still learning English. She decided to try writing in English. She started writing a story about a young woman from China who was living in London and learning English.

one-third one out of three
was surrounded by the area around

▶ **Before You Continue**

1. **Clarify** What difficulties did Xiaolu have when she first moved to England?
2. **Compare/Contrast** What changed for Xiaolu when she moved to London?

When Xiaolu turned 30, she decided to have a birthday party. She had never done this before—in China, most families do not celebrate birthdays. She invited her friends and made **dumplings** and other traditional Chinese dishes.

In China, Xiaolu had thought that people became very old after they turned 30. But in England, her friends had different ideas. "Thirty is a good age," they told her. "It is when you start **achieving your goals**."

Xiaolu thought about her goals: the films she wanted to make, the books she wanted to write, the places she still wanted to see. Would these goals soon become reality?

dumplings Chinese food made from meat and flour

achieving your goals doing things you always wanted to do

Xiaolu's scholarship **supported** her to stay in England for one year. However, after a few months in London, she decided that she wanted to stay in England for a longer period. Without her scholarship, she needed a new way to make money. She decided to try to **publish** her story, even though her English wasn't perfect. Her story was about a woman learning English, so the mistakes made it more **authentic**.

She was surprised when she was invited to meet a group of editors at a publishing company.

"We want to publish your book!" they told her. Xiaolu was very happy. The publishing company paid her enough money for her to continue living in England.

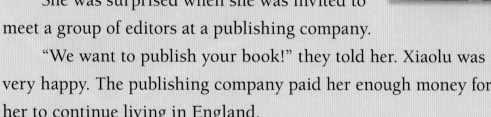

supported provided money for
publish print
authentic real

▶ **Before You Continue**
1. **Clarify** Why did Xiaolu decide to publish her book?
2. **Compare/Contrast** What are some differences between birthdays in China and in England?

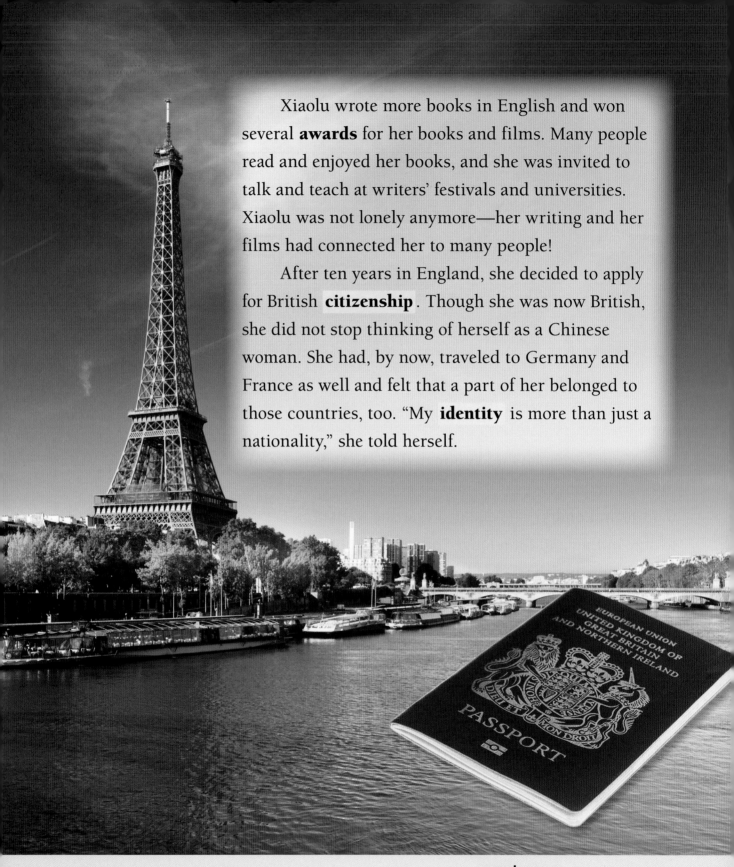

Xiaolu wrote more books in English and won several **awards** for her books and films. Many people read and enjoyed her books, and she was invited to talk and teach at writers' festivals and universities. Xiaolu was not lonely anymore—her writing and her films had connected her to many people!

After ten years in England, she decided to apply for British **citizenship**. Though she was now British, she did not stop thinking of herself as a Chinese woman. She had, by now, traveled to Germany and France as well and felt that a part of her belonged to those countries, too. "My **identity** is more than just a nationality," she told herself.

awards prizes

When Xiaolu turned 40 in 2013, she gave birth to her daughter. Xiaolu thought about her own childhood in China, when she had lived in the fishing village with her grandparents. Born in London, her baby would have a very different life. Like Xiaolu, she would be British with a Chinese background. But what would the baby learn about Chinese culture by growing up in the West?

Xiaolu decided to visit her family in China so they could meet her new baby. She had not been back to China for many years and had never seen her father's **grave**. She went for the Qingming Festival, which is a special time to **honor** the dead.

Xiaolu wanted to tell the story of her move to England, of **adapting** to living and writing in a new language, and of learning the **customs** of her new country. She also wanted her family to know about her life since she had left, what it was like to live in England, and how she had changed.

So, in 2017, she wrote her story, and it became a very popular book called *Once Upon a Time in the East: A Story of Growing Up.* ❖

▲ **The Qingming Festival is a Chinese custom to honor the dead.**

grave burial place
honor remember

▶**Before You Continue**

1. **Clarify** Why did Xiaolu decide to visit her family in China?
2. **Compare/Contrast** Xiaolu believes that her daughter's life will be very different from her own. Why does she believe this?

Think and Respond

Talk About It

Key Words

adapt	ethnic
challenge	foreign
citizenship	identity
custom	origin
diversity	society

1. What do you think Xiaolu Guo is like, based on her **biography**? Provide evidence from the text.

2. Imagine that you could meet Xiaolu Guo. What **questions** would you **ask** her?

3. What are some different ways in which words and writing are important to Xiaolu Guo? Find some examples in the text.

Write About It

What do you think is the biggest **challenge** in **adapting** to life in a **foreign** country? Write a paragraph about your thoughts. Use **Key Words** to explain your thinking.

I think _____ is challenging because _____ .

Compare and Contrast

Compare and contrast Xiaolu Guo's life in China and her life in England.

Venn Diagram

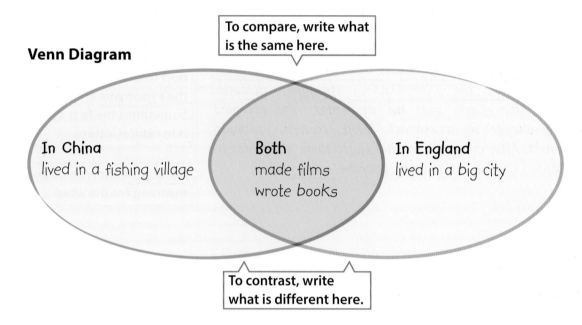

To compare, write what is the same here.

In China
lived in a fishing village

Both
made films
wrote books

In England
lived in a big city

To contrast, write what is different here.

Now use your diagram to retell the story of Xiaolu Guo's life to a partner. Use as many **Key Words** as you can.

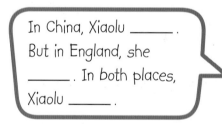

In China, Xiaolu _____ .
But in England, she _____ . In both places, Xiaolu _____ .

Fluency

Practice reading with expression. Rate your reading.

Talk Together

How did Xiaolu Guo have to change to fit in to life in England? Write a poem about Xiaolu's move. Include **Key Words** in your poem. Share your poem with the class.

Use a Thesaurus

A **thesaurus** lists synonyms and antonyms. Synonyms are words with almost the same meaning. Antonyms are words with opposite meanings.

Read this entry from a thesaurus.

challenge noun **1.** *Judy thinks that Math is a real challenge for her.* DIFFICULTY, struggle, obstacle, trial **2.** *After Carla beat me at tennis, she accepted my challenge to a rematch.* DARE, contest, invitation ▶ verb **1.** *After the game, we challenged them to a rematch.* DEMAND, dare, invite, confront, provoke ANTONYM avoid

> A **sample sentence** shows how to use the word. Then the **synonyms** are shown. Sometimes the first synonym is in capital letters.

> **Antonyms** show an opposite meaning for the word.

Try It Together

Read the thesaurus entry. Then answer the questions.

adapt verb **1.** *It took me more than a year to adapt to living in the United States.* ADJUST, conform, change, fit in **2.** *The writer adapted the book to make it easier for children.* REWORK, modify, redo, edit ANTONYM stay the same, maintain

1. **Which word is an antonym for adapt?**

   A rework

   B maintain

   C easier

   D adjust

2. **Which words are synonyms?**

   A fit in, rework

   B adapt, rework

   C adapt, maintain

   D adjust, comfortable

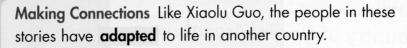

Migrant Stories from Around the World

by Penelope McKimm

People choose to move to a different country for many different reasons. Some are looking for a better **economic opportunity**. Others hope that moving to a new country will help them have safer, more peaceful lives. Some want to go to college or learn new **skills**. Others simply want to explore the world and learn a new language and culture.

There are some international organizations that collect migration stories from all over the world. People are invited to share their stories and offer advice. Here are four stories of people who have each moved to a different country. They tell us about the reasons why people migrate, the problems they **face**, and how they feel in their new countries.

economic opportunity chance to make money
skills abilities
face have, encounter

▸ **Before You Continue**
1. **Clarify** What will these stories describe?
2. **Make Inferences** What kind of work do you think the International Organization for Migration does?

Luis
Country of Origin: *Argentina*
Moved to: *United States*

United States

Argentina

Luis moved to the United States after he was given a scholarship to study at a university in New York, where most people speak English. Although Luis knew some English, he often found it difficult to communicate.

Being far away from his family and friends was also a **challenge** for Luis. It made him feel sad to **miss out on** birthdays and other important events in his family. However, he found New York a very interesting and beautiful city and **gradually** began to think of it as his home.

"I have achieved a level of independence and developed some personal skills that perhaps I wouldn't have acquired in my country," he says.

Luis enjoys the **diversity** in New York, where he has met people from all over the world.

miss out on not be there for
gradually slowly

Elsa
Country of Origin: *Portugal*
Moved to: *Guatemala*

Elsa says that although all of her family is from Portugal, she feels **at home** in a tropical climate.

Guatemala Portugal

Elsa moved to Guatemala for her work. Although she originally planned to stay for only one year, she soon realized that she loved Guatemala so much that she wanted to live there **permanently**. She especially loved the hot weather and was fascinated by Guatemalan traditions and **customs** . For Elsa, one of the most difficult parts of **adapting** to life in Guatemala was driving!

Elsa works for an international organization that helps improve the lives of children in Guatemala. She loves her work.

"The most beautiful thing that Guatemala has given me is the opportunity to meet great people who have become great friends," she says.

at home comfortable
permanently always

▶ **Before You Continue**
1. **Make Inferences** Why do you think driving in Guatemala is difficult?
2. **Use Text Features** How do you know whose words are quoted on each page?

Kossi originally planned to go to Algeria, but then he decided to go to Cameroon and work as a mechanic.

Kossi
Country of Origin: *Togo*
Moved to: *Cameroon*

"You will **rarely** see a Togolese leave his country," says Kossi. However, after arriving in Cameroon, he was very surprised to discover that there were many other Togolese already living there! Interested in helping his community, he spoke to the **mayor** of the city where he lived about creating a Togolese association. The mayor accepted the offer, and after it was announced on the radio, nearly 200 people joined the association.

Kossi wanted to do more to help people. So he went to work for an international organization for migrant people, giving assistance to other migrants and their families, listening to their stories, and offering advice and **comfort**.

rarely not usually
mayor the elected leader of a city or town
comfort help

"I've been welcomed so warmly by Estonians," Sophie says. "I probably won't be able to repay all this kindness, but I would like to give the society something back in the future."

Sophie
Country of Origin: *Australia*
Moved to: *Estonia*

When she first arrived in Estonia, it took Sophie some time to make friends. "It's hard to get close to people, but once you do, the friendship is forever," she says. Even though she has been living in Estonia for some time, Sophie has not yet learned Estonian. Many people in her city speak English very well, and Sophie has found that she can **get by** with English most of the time.

However, Sophie believes that learning Estonian will help her become more **integrated**. She wants to be able to read the local newspaper and attend cultural events as a way to become closer to the people around her. ❖

get by do what she needs to do
integrated part of the community

▶ **Before You Continue**
1. **Clarify** What does Sophie see as her biggest **challenge** in Estonia?
2. **Generalize** What experiences are shared by Luis, Elsa, Kossi, and Sophie?

Respond and Extend

Key Words

adapt	ethnic
challenge	foreign
citizenship	identity
custom	origin
diversity	society

Compare Literary Language

In "Migrant Stories from Around the World," the author talks about the people's experiences in a direct way. She gives short descriptions of facts and directly reports words spoken. In "A Writer's Journey," the author describes the experiences in a narrative way, with more personal details such as feelings and thoughts.

Compare how language is used for the different styles. Work with a partner to complete the chart.

Comparison Chart

	"A Writer's Journey"	"Migrant Stories from Around the World"
People		"It's hard to get close to people, but once you do, the friendship is forever," she says.
Events		
Places	Instead of big, beautiful houses, she saw short, gray buildings against the dark sky.	

Talk Together

Think about Xiaolu Guo and the participants in "Migrant Stories from Around the World." What do they think of life in their new countries? Use **Key Words** to talk about your ideas.

Compound Subjects

A **compound subject** has two or more simple subjects. The simple subjects are often joined by **and** or **or**. The <u>subject</u> and <u>verb</u> of a sentence must agree.

Grammar Rules Compound Subjects	
Compound Subject	**Subject-Verb Agreement**
• Use a <u>plural verb</u> when **two** <u>subjects</u> are joined by *and*.	<u>Xiaolu</u> and <u>her family</u> <u>were</u> very excited.
• If the subjects are joined by *or*, look at the last subject.	
▫ If the **last subject** is singular, use a <u>singular verb</u>.	More jobs or **a better way of** <u>life</u> <u>brings</u> people to America.
▫ If the **last subject** is plural, use a <u>plural verb</u>.	A better way of life or **more** <u>jobs</u> <u>bring</u> people to America.

Read Compound Subjects

Read this short paragraph. Find the compound subject. Does it use a singular or a plural verb?

"I like Guatemala very much. The climate and the people make me feel very comfortable and happy. I feel very much at home in the tropics."

Write Compound Subjects

Choose two people from "Migrant Stories from Around the World." Write two sentences about them. Use a compound subject in each sentence. Be sure that the subject and verb agree. Share your sentences with a partner.

Write About Yourself

Write a Personal Narrative

Write about a time when you had to adjust to a new place or situation. Add your story to a class book about dealing with change.

Study a Model

A personal narrative is a true story about something that happened to you.

The beginning tells you what the event is all about.

My First American Supermarket
by Eric Tran

My family moved to the U.S. from Vietnam. At first, everything in the U.S. seemed really strange, especially the supermarket!

In Vietnam, we shopped at the market. All the food was outdoors in stalls and carts. We bought rice noodles, farm-fresh vegetables, and fish.

The writer compares two settings and gives plenty of examples to develop the main idea.

Our first trip to the American supermarket was a shock! All the food was on shelves inside a building. The fish was wrapped in plastic. The vegetables were canned or frozen.

The ending tells you why the experience was important.

I miss our old market. But, the American store has good food, too, such as pizza and yogurt. So, I guess something can be different and still be really good!

Prewrite

1. **Choose a Topic** What experience will you write about? Talk with a partner to choose an event that was important to you.

Language Frames	
Tell Your Ideas	**Respond to Ideas**
The biggest change I ever had was _____ .	Tell me why _____ was so important to you.
I remember when I _____ .	How did you feel about _____ ?
One thing that happened to me was _____ .	I'd like to read more about _____ because _____ .

> Use sentences like these to help you choose a topic.

2. **Gather Information** Collect details that describe where and when your event took place. Write down your feelings before and after. Say how the experience affected you.

3. **Get Organized** Use a T-Chart to help you organize your details.

T-Chart

Vietnam	United States
-Vietnamese market	-U.S. supermarket
-outside	-inside a building

Draft

Use your T-Chart to write your draft. Explain what happened and how the experience affected you. Give plenty of examples to develop your ideas.

Revise

1. **Read, Retell, Respond** Read your draft aloud to a partner. Your partner listens and then retells the story. Next, talk about ways to improve your writing.

Language Frames

Retell

- Your experience was mostly about _____ .

- At the beginning, you felt _____ . At the end, you felt _____ .

- The experience was important to you because _____ .

Make Suggestions

- I can't really picture _____ . Can you add more details?

- Why is _____ something you remember so well?

- Can you add more details about _____ ?

> Use sentences like these to respond to your partner's writing.

---

2. **Make Changes** Think about your draft and your partner's suggestions. Then use revision marks to make your changes.

- Did you develop your ideas with details and examples? Add more details if you need to.

> All the food was stacked on shelves inside a building.
> Our first trip to the American supermarket was a shock! ∧

- Did you include how the event affected you or changed your ideas? Replace or add words to make the change clear.

> But, the American store has good food, too, such as pizza and yogurt. ~~I feel OK about that now.~~ ⌐ So, I guess something can
> be different and still be
> really good!

Grammar Tip

For subjects connected by *or*, use a verb that agrees with the subject closest to it.

Edit and Proofread

Work with a partner to edit and proofread your personal narrative. Pay special attention to subject-verb agreement. Use revision marks to show your changes.

Present

On Your Own Make a final copy of your personal narrative. Choose a way to share it with your classmates. You can read it aloud, or retell the story as though you were telling your younger brother or sister.

Presentation Tips	
If you are the speaker...	**If you are the listener...**
For some parts of your story, change your voice to show how you were feeling.	Listen for details that help you picture what the speaker is describing.
Use gestures if they feel natural.	Make connections to similar experiences in your own life.

In a Group Collect all the personal narratives from your class. Bind them into a book, and work together to think of a good title. You may want to add clip art or scan in a photograph to add interest to your own story.

BIG Question

?

How can where you are change who you are?

Talk Together

In this unit, you found lots of answers to the **Big Question**. Now, use your concept map to discuss the **Big Question** with the class.

Concept Map

What I eat

What I wear

How can where you are change who you are?

How I speak

How I see myself

Before I wore only dresses and skirts. Now I wear only jeans!

Write a Diary Entry ✏

Use your concept map to choose one change that happens to people when they move to a new place. Choose a person from this unit. Write a diary entry about how that person handled the change you have chosen.

Share Your Ideas

Choose one of these ways to share your ideas about the **Big Question**.

Write It!

Write a Letter

Write a letter or an e-mail to a pen pal in a foreign country. Ask questions to find out what life is like in his or her country. Tell your pen pal about life in your country.

Talk About It!

Create a Documentary

Choose a classmate to interview. Ask for information about his or her life. Use the information to sketch a simple story board showing important events. Then use those events to make a documentary about your classmate.

Do It!

Give a Tour

Pretend you and your classmates are tour guides. Make a list of places in your school that newcomers should know about. Write about the places. Then take your classmates on a tour of those places.

Write It!

Make a Collage

Make a collage that shows the different ways one of the people you read about changed and remained the same. Write a caption that names the person and explains why you chose the items.

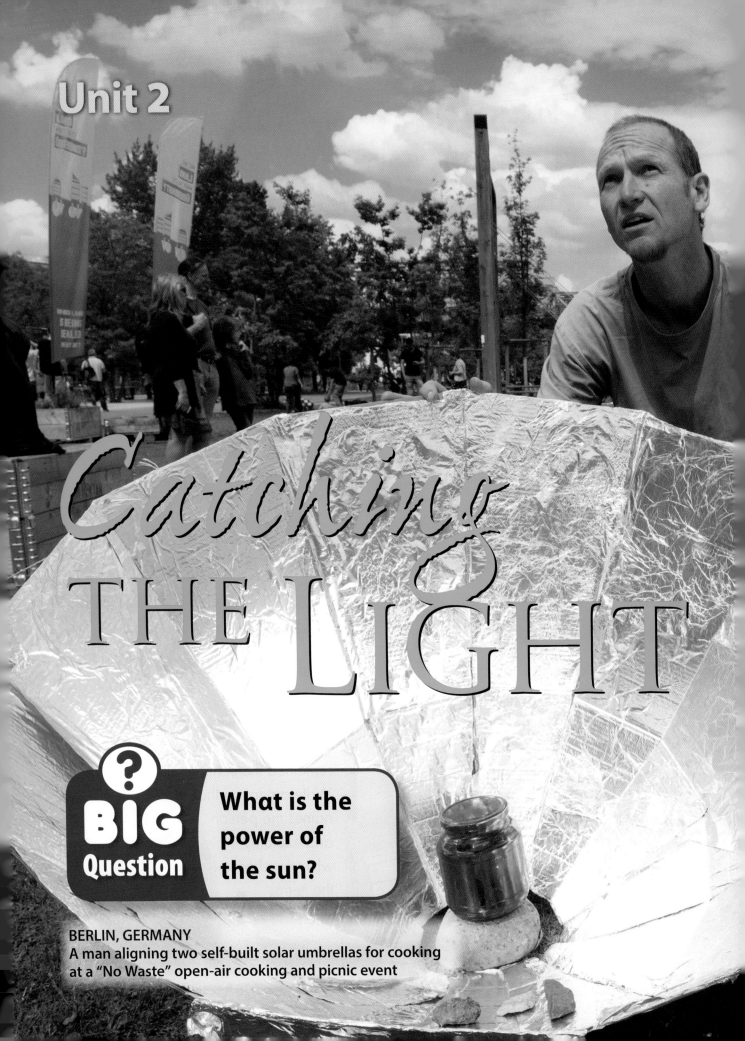

Unit 2

Catching THE LIGHT

BIG Question

What is the power of the sun?

BERLIN, GERMANY
A man aligning two self-built solar umbrellas for cooking at a "No Waste" open-air cooking and picnic event

Share What You Know

Do It!

❶ **Think** of words that describe the sun. Make a list.

❷ **Choose a word** from your list and draw it.

❸ **Share your drawing** with the class.

sunny
warm
bright

Give and Carry Out Commands

Listen to Alfredo and Susana's song. Then use **Language Frames** to give commands to a partner. Have your partner restate the commands before doing them.

Song

Make Sun Tea

How I want some iced tea, Susana, Susana,
Will you make some for me, Susana my friend?

You can make tea with sunlight, Alfredo, Alfredo,
In an hour it's done right, Alfredo my friend.

Put tea bags in water, Alfredo, Alfredo,
It gets hotter and hotter, Alfredo my friend.

Then you put in some fresh ice, Alfredo, Alfredo,
And the iced tea is quite nice, Alfredo my friend.

Give the pitcher to me, Susana, Susana,
And I'll make the iced tea, Susana my friend.

Tune: "There's a Hole in the Bucket"

pitcher

Key Words

absorb

heat

reflect

thermal

transmit

🔊 Key Words

Look at this illustration. Use **Key Words** to talk about how the sun **transmits** energy.

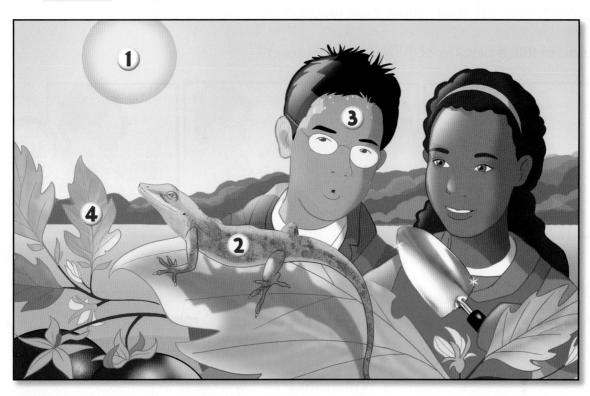

1. The sun transmits energy, or sunlight.

2. Plants, animals, and objects can **reflect** or **absorb** the sunlight.

3. Light that is absorbed can change into **thermal** energy, or **heat**.

4. Plants change sunlight into food.

Talk Together

How do plants and animals use the power of the sun? With a group, use **Key Words** to describe what a day in your life might be like without any sunshine at all.

Character

When you think about the conflict, or problem, that **characters** in a story face, you often think about their roles, or parts they play, in the conflict. You also think about their functions, or what they do.

Look at these pictures of Alfredo and Susana.

Map and Talk

You can use a character chart to describe characters' roles and functions in a conflict. Here's how you make one.

Write each character's role here.

Write each character's function here.

Character Chart

Character	Role	Function	Conflict
Alfredo	learner	tries to get Susana to make tea for him	Susana wants Alfredo to make the tea.
Susana	teacher	tries to teach Alfredo to make sun tea	Alfredo wants Susana to make the tea.

Write each character's name here.

Write each character's conflict here.

Talk **Together**

With a partner, think of a story with a conflict. Use a character chart to show each character's role and function in the conflict.

🔊 More Key Words

Use these words to talk about "Ten Suns" and "How the Fifth Sun Came to Be."

assume
verb

When you **assume** something, you think it is true without checking the facts.

event
noun

An **event** is something that happens. The street fair is a big **event**.

explanation
noun

An **explanation** gives a reason or makes something easy to understand.

power
noun

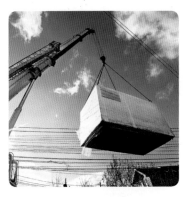

Power is strength or energy. This machine has the **power** to lift heavy things.

theory
noun

A **theory** is an idea that explains something. Her **theory** is that the dog did it.

Talk Together

Work with a partner. Write a question using a **Key Word**. Answer the question using a different **Key Word**. Use all the words twice.

Question: What is a theory?

Answer: an explanation of something.

Learn to Ask Questions

Look at the cartoon. When you wonder or get confused about something, you usually **ask a question** and then try to find the answer.

total eclipse of the sun

When you read, you can **ask questions**, too. The answers to some questions can be found **in the story**. Read to find the answers. This will help you understand the story better.

How to Ask Questions

?	1. As you read, ask a question.	I wonder _____ .
👁	2. Look for an answer in the text. You might find the answer right there in the text, or you might have to think and search.	I read _____ . So _____ .
📖	3. Think about the answer. Read on and ask more questions.	Now I wonder _____ .

Talk Together

Read Susana's story. Read the sample. Use **Language Frames** to ask questions. Tell a partner about them.

Science Fiction

How the Sun Got Hot Again

Astronauts Sofie and Karl were ready to go into space. They were on a special mission. The sun had been growing colder every day. It was getting harder and harder to survive on Earth.

Sofie had an **explanation**. A **thermal** force deep inside the sun had stopped working. If her **theory** was right, setting off a huge explosion on the sun's surface should strengthen its **power**.

"I wonder what is happening to the sun.

I read that a thermal force has stopped working.

So now I know what happened.

Now I wonder if their mission will succeed."

The spaceship took off. Before long, the sun was a huge ball right in front of them. It was as majestic as they had imagined it. "The **heat** shields on our spaceship are working," Sofie noted. ◀

"We'd melt if they weren't," Karl said nervously. Soon, it was time to send off the explosives. Sofie pressed a button. The little ship holding the explosives made its way to the sun. ◀

Sofie turned the big ship around. They needed to get far from the sun before the explosion. KA-BOOM! The shock waves rocked the spaceship. Sofie spoke to Mission Control. "It worked!" she cried.

"Excellent!!" Karl exclaimed. "I **assume** that tomorrow's headlines will read: 'Astronauts Saved the Sun!' This **event** will go down in history!"

◀ = a good place to stop and ask a question

Read a Story

Genre

A **myth** is a very old story. Its purpose is to explain something about the world. Myths often include gods and characters who have special powers, but who act in human ways.

Point of View

Point of view describes who tells a story. In the third-person point of view, a narrator outside of the story tells the story. The narrator uses words like *he*, *she*, or *they* to explain what characters experience, think, and feel.

But the gratitude of the earth's people and the importance of their work meant nothing to the boys. They found their task boring.

Ten Suns

A Chinese Myth

retold by **Eric A. Kimmel** • illustrated by **Marilee Heyer**

▶ **Set a Purpose**
Find out about an unusual
family who lives in the sky.

Long ago, when the world was new, a giant mulberry tree grew on the far side of the sea, on the edge of the **eastern horizon**. Its roots plunged deep into the earth. Its branches scraped the sky.

Nestled in the topmost branches of this tree stood a **jade** palace. Hammered sheets of gold formed its roof. Its windows were made of the thinnest **panes of amethyst and lapis lazuli**. This was the palace of Di Jun, the eastern emperor, the god who ruled the regions of the sky where the sun arises.

eastern horizon the land where the sun rises
jade green stone
◀ **panes of amethyst and lapis lazuli** purple and blue crystal

In those days, there were ten suns: the children of Di Jun and his wife, Xi He. They never walked across the sky together. That would produce too much **heat** for the world to **bear**. Instead, every morning before dawn, Xi He would awaken one of her sons. They would climb into her dragon chariot and drive to a point on the eastern horizon where Xi He's son would begin his walk.

bear survive

Each day, one of the suns would walk across the sky from east to west. When the people on Earth saw the sun crossing the heavens, bringing warmth and light, they offered thanks to Di Jun, Xi He, and their family.

But the **gratitude** of the earth's people and the importance of their work meant nothing to the boys. They **found their task** boring. Day after day, year after year, century after century, they followed the same path across the sky. There was no one to talk to, nothing new to see, nothing to do except follow that same **weary track** over and over again.

One night, as Di Jun's boys lay in bed, they began talking. Huo Feng Huang, the oldest, said, "I would not mind walking the path so much if I **had some company**."

gratitude thankfulness
found their task thought their job was
weary track old path
had some company was not alone

"I feel the same way," Pi Li Xing, the youngest, replied. "Tomorrow, let's do something different. Why don't we all get up early, take the dragon chariot, and walk across the sky together?"

The others agreed. "A splendid idea!"

In the dark of night, while their parents slept, the boys **arose**, put on their brightest **garments**, **hitched** the dragon to their mother's chariot, and rode across the star-swept sky to the eastern horizon. Laughing, chattering, with their arms around one another's shoulders, they began their walk.

arose got out of bed
garments clothes
hitched connected

▶ **Before You Continue**

1. **Ask Questions** Why are the children called both *suns* and *sons* in the story? Where can you find the answer?

2. **Character/Plot** What is the role of the sons in the story? What is their conflict?

▶ **Predict**
What will happen to Earth when the sons cross the sky together?

When dawn came, the people who lived on Earth were **astonished** to see ten suns appear above the horizon. The blazing **heat** of ten suns shining down at once was more than the world could bear. Crops **withered** in the fields. Forests caught fire. Lakes and rivers dried up. Mountains shattered to pieces. The sea began to boil. People and animals grew **faint**. They stretched themselves on the **scorching** ground and waited to die.

astonished very surprised
withered dried up and died
faint weak and dizzy
scorching burning hot

The great emperor Shun, who ruled the nations of the world, cried to the eastern god Di Jun.

"Why are you punishing us? What have the creatures of Earth done to deserve this terrible **fate**? Have we not followed the proper **rites**? Have we not offered the correct **sacrifices**? Why have you sent your sons to destroy us?"

fate ending
rites ceremonies
sacrifices gifts to the gods

The great emperor's cries woke Di Jun and Xi He. They looked out the window of the jade palace. In the distance, they saw their ten sons marching together across the sky. Di Jun and Xi He called to them, "Come back at once! Go no further!"

But the boys did not listen. Earth was far below. They could not see the damage they were causing. Higher and higher they climbed, until they reached the place where the sun stands at noon.

Di Jun could not allow the world to be destroyed. The **existence** of all living things depended on him. If his sons would not **abandon their reckless walk**, he would have to stop them. Di Jun **summoned** Hou Yi, the Archer of Heaven.

existence survival
abandon their reckless walk stop walking across the sky
summoned called for

Hou Yi had once been a man. He introduced the science of archery to the world by inventing the bow and arrow. As a reward for his discovery, the gods placed him in the heavens among the **constellations**.

Di Jun presented Hou Yi with a magic bow and ten magic arrows. With tears filling his eyes, he told Hou Yi, "Shoot down the ten suns—my sons—who are burning up the earth."

constellations stars

▶ **Before You Continue**
1. **Ask Questions** Look at the picture of Hou Yi. What questions could you ask about him?
2. **Character/Plot** What conflict does Di Jun face? How does he work to solve it?

Hou Yi **refused**. "How can I harm your boys? They are like my children. I taught them to shoot with a bow and arrow. We both still love them, even when they **disobey**."

"I love the creatures of Earth, too. I must protect them," Di Jun told Hou Yi. "Do not be afraid. You will not harm the boys. My sons will not be hurt, but they will be changed. Never again will they cross the sky as suns. They will be gods no more. Hurry! Do as I command. **There is no time to spare**. Earth is dying."

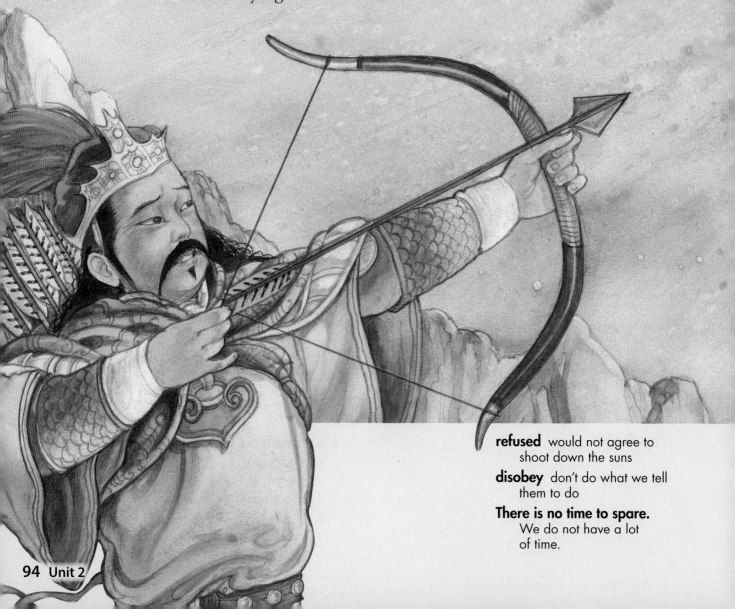

refused would not agree to shoot down the suns

disobey don't do what we tell them to do

There is no time to spare. We do not have a lot of time.

Hou Yi took Di Jun's bow and magic arrows. He rode the wind down to Earth. Taking his place on top of White Mountain, he planted his feet firmly and took careful aim. Hou Yi released the bowstring. The magic arrow **streaked** across the sky. It struck the first of the ten suns, shattering it to pieces.

One by one, Hou Yi's arrows **found their mark**. Each sun exploded, filling the sky with **blinding** light. The boys fell to Earth, but they did not die. Instead, they turned into black-feathered birds. They became crows.

streaked flew
found their mark hit their targets
blinding very bright

95

The emperor Shun watched the suns exploding in the sky. Suddenly he realized that if Hou Yi destroyed all the suns, there would be no **heat** or light. The earth would **be plunged into** icy darkness.

There was no time to **spare**. The emperor Shun summoned his fastest messenger.

"Go to the top of White Mountain. Find Hou Yi. Remove one arrow from his **quiver** to make sure he does not shoot down all the suns."

be plunged into suddenly become a place of
spare wait
◄ **quiver** bag of arrows

The messenger **mounted** his horse. He rode faster than he had ever ridden in his life, all the way to the top of White Mountain. There he saw Hou Yi. By now, only one sun remained in the sky. Shun's messenger **plucked** the last arrow from Hou Yi's quiver just as the Archer of Heaven reached for it. Finding no more magic arrows, Hou Yi **assumed** his work was done. He unstrung his bow and rode the wind back to the stars.

mounted climbed onto
plucked took

Since that day, only one sun shines overhead. Every morning, the crows gather on White Mountain to greet the dawn. *"Gua! Gua!"* they call to their brother, the sun, as he begins his lonely walk across the sky.

For they remember that once, they too were gods and hope for the day when their parents, Di Jun and Xi He, will forgive them. ❖

▶ **Before You Continue**

1. **Character/Plot** Who saves Earth, and how does he or she save it?
2. **Genre** What things in nature does this myth explain?

Meet the Author

Eric A. Kimmel

Eric A. Kimmel says that his greatest love is to share stories from different countries and cultures. It must be true, because he has retold over fifty tales from around the world! He often travels to different countries, and he is always looking for story ideas.

In China, Eric visited the Forbidden City, where Chinese emperors lived hundreds of years ago. There, the most important buildings face toward the east, to honor the Sun.

◄ Eric Kimmel likes to travel the world in search of story ideas.

Writing Tip

The author doesn't just say that the suns were hot. Instead, he uses words like "blazing," "scorching," and "blinding" to describe them. Such vivid words make the myth more exciting for the reader. Write a description of the moon rising in the sky. Use vivid words to describe its light.

Think and Respond

Talk About It

Key Words

absorb	power
assume	reflect
event	theory
explanation	thermal
heat	transmit

1. Describe two elements of the story that make it a **myth**.

I know "Ten Suns" is a myth because _____ .

2. Imagine that you are Di Jun. **Give commands** to a messenger. Say what he must do in order to save the world. Use your own words.

Go _____ . Then _____ .

3. Tell a partner about a part of the story that you thought was hard to understand. Explain how you asked yourself questions to understand it better.

I wondered _____ .
I read _____ . So _____ .
Then I wondered _____ .

Write About It

Do you think that Di Jun made the right decision about his sons? Write a paragraph that explains your answer. Include details from the myth in your **explanation** . Use **Key Words**.

I think that Di Jun _____ .
One reason I think that is _____ . Another reason is that _____ .

Character

With a partner, discuss the characters and the conflict in "Ten Suns." Then make a character chart to talk about the characters' roles and functions in the conflict.

Character Chart

> Write the characters' roles here.

> Write the characters' functions here.

> Write the characters' roles in the conflict here.

Character	Role	Function	Conflict
Di Jun	father		His sons want to light the sky all at once.
ten suns			

With your partner, use the chart to describe the characters and what happens to them. Use the sentence frames and **Key Words**. Record your retelling.

> Di Jun's conflict is with his sons. He wants _____. But his sons want _____.

Fluency

Practice reading with intonation. Rate your reading.

Talk Together

How did the sons misuse their **power**? Draw a picture showing what happened. Use **Key Words** as labels. Share your picture with the class.

Word Origins

Many English words include a **root** that came from another language. When you come to a word you don't know, look for a root to help you determine the meaning of the word.

This chart shows some common roots.

Root	Origin	Meaning	Example
graph	Greek	write	auto**graph** , para**graph**
cred	Latin	believe	**cred**ible, **cred**it
wis, wit	Old English	know	**wis**dom, **wit**ness

If *auto* means *self*, and the Greek root *graph* means *write*, what do you think the word *autograph* means?

Try It Together

Read the paragraph. Then answer the questions. Use the chart to help you.

> Characters in myths often possess great <u>wisdom</u>. Others can be reckless. Though it seems <u>incredible</u>, in the myth "Ten Suns," a father must sacrifice his sons to save the world from disaster.

1. **Look for the Old English root in the word *wisdom*. What do you think *wisdom* means?**

   A damaged

   B without care

   C knowledge

   D proved something to be true

2. **Look for the Latin root *cred*. What do you think <u>incredible</u> means?**

   A caused by heat

   B hard to believe

   C relating to three

   D stories or myths

Making Connections You read a Chinese myth about the Sun. Now read another myth from the Aztecs of Mexico.

Genre An **origin myth** is a very old story that explains how something in nature came to be. Most origin myths reflect the values of a particular culture.

How the Fifth Sun Came to Be
AN AZTEC MYTH

retold by Lulu Delacre
illustrated by Rafael López

*The Aztec people lived long ago in Mexico. Their culture was rich with traditional stories and myths. Aztec storytellers may have **passed down** these stories by chanting or singing them.*

passed down taught

▶ **Before You Continue**

1. **Genre** What **event** in nature do you think this myth will be about?
2. **Ask Questions** Based on the introduction, what questions do you have about Aztec storytellers?

THE JAGUAR SUN

THE WIND SUN

In the times before **the current era**, there had been four worlds. Each time a new world was created, it was destroyed. The gods Tezcatlipoca and Quetzalcoatl were in constant battle to become the ruling sun of each world.

The first world was ruled by Tezcatlipoca, the **Jaguar** Sun. Under his rule, jaguars roamed the earth until they **devoured** all the people. This brought an end to the first world and let Quetzalcoatl become the second sun, the Wind Sun.

The Wind Sun ruled the second world and life on Earth returned. Then, wanting to rule again, Tezcatlipoca kicked Quetzalcoatl from the throne. Their conflict caused giant **hurricanes** to destroy the second world.

the current era today's world
◀ **Jaguar** Great Cat
devoured ate
hurricanes wind storms

THE RAIN SUN

THE WATER SUN

Quetzalcoatl returned and **selected** another god to become the third sun, the Rain Sun. Animals, plants, and humans again returned to the earth. But one day, Quetzalcoatl, being jealous of the Rain Sun's successful rule, sent a rain of fire that poured over everything. Blazing fireballs **charred** every home, animal, and plant, leaving only blackness **in their wake**.

Quetzalcoatl then chose a new god to become the Water Sun, ruler of the fourth world. For a while, things went well. Then the sky fell to the earth and a great flood swept away all human life. **Thus** ended the fourth world.

selected chose
charred burned
in their wake wherever they had been
Thus That was what

▶ **Before You Continue**

1. **Generalize** How did the Aztecs explain natural disasters, such as floods and hurricanes? Give an example.

2. **Compare Characters** What roles do Quetzalcoatl and Tezcatlipoca play in the story? What is their conflict?

So it was that Quetzalcoatl **took it upon himself to** bring back the human race for the last time. He traveled far to find a way to populate the earth with men, women, and children once again. Once he brought back the people, he realized that the earth was still dark in an eternal night. A bitter cold enveloped it. No plants would grow without warmth and light, and animals and humans would go hungry.

Therefore, when the gods were called to a meeting in **sacred Teotihuacán**, Quetzalcoatl was first to arrive. There, surrounded by huge stone pyramids, burned the divine **hearth**. For a long time, the spirits talked until they reached an agreement. They pointed to Nanahuatl, the most **humble** of the gods.

took it upon himself to decided that he would
sacred Teotihuacán the city of the gods
hearth fireplace
humble modest; respectful

"You, Nanahuatl," they spoke, "must take care of the sky and the earth. You must **sacrifice** yourself to become the sun!"

So, Nanahuatl closed his eyes, **braced himself**, and leaped into the blazing fire. The fire sputtered and flared, its flames rising high into the sky.

Then, another spirit, who also **yearned** to be the sun, followed Nanahuatl's steps and jumped into the center of the swaying flames. When both spirits were gone, the gods sat down to wait for Nanahuatl's appearance in the sky. They knew he would become the fifth sun.

sacrifice give up
braced himself got ready
yearned wished

▶ **Before You Continue**
1. **Character** How does Quetzalcoatl's role change?
2. **Make Inferences** Why do you think the gods choose a humble god to become the new sun?

They looked to the north and they looked to the south. They looked to the west and they looked to the east. But the sky remained as dark and the earth as cold as before. It was Quetzalcoatl who spoke next. "It will rise from the east," he said.

In an instant, the whole sky became **crimson** and gold. The **spectacle** was so glorious that the gods believed the sun was rising from everywhere.

As dawn defined itself, they saw the new sun clearly rising from the east, blinding with its brilliance. Its rays reached farther and farther as it moved in its path, painting valleys and mountains, rivers and lakes, in its golden light. Then the gods noticed the second spirit who had jumped into the fire. He was now a faint moon, following the **majestic** sun.

crimson deep red
spectacle show of light
As dawn defined itself In the morning light
majestic marvelous and brilliant

It is said that the gods **knelt** at the sight of this spectacular fifth sun and gave praises to its **power**. They saw how its warmth affected seeds and made plants grow. They saw how its rays made water rise and pour back down in the form of light rain.

Now the people of the earth would live and **prosper**. And that was good.

According to the ancient Aztec calendar stone, we still live in the fifth world, ruled by the **Sun of Movement**. ❖

Aztec Calendar Stone

This is a drawing of the center part of the Aztec Calendar Stone, which was discovered in Mexico City in 1790. It shows the gods representing the five worlds. The fifth god is at the center.

knelt got on their knees
prosper do well
Sun of Movement Fifth Sun

▶ **Before You Continue**

1. **Ask Questions** What question do you have about the god who became the moon?

2. **Imagery** How does the author's description of the new sun help you understand its **power**?

Respond and Extend

Key Words

absorb	power
assume	reflect
event	theory
explanation	thermal
heat	transmit

Compare Myths

"Ten Suns" and "How the Fifth Sun Came to Be" are **origin myths**. Work with a partner to fill in the chart below. Then talk about how the myths are alike and how they are different.

Comparison Chart

	"Ten Suns"	"How the Fifth Sun Came to Be"
The type of myth		Aztec
What the myth explains		
Setting		Mexico
The characters	Gods: Heroes: Other:	Gods: Heroes: Other:
What the story is about	Beginning: Middle: End:	Beginning: Middle: End:
The story's message		

Talk Together

Think about the two selections and the chart above. How do the two myths help you understand the importance of the Sun? Use **Key Words** to discuss your ideas.

Kinds of Sentences

There are **four kinds of sentences**.

Grammar Rules Kinds of Sentences	
A **statement** tells something.	This myth is about gods and heroes.
A **command** tells you to do something.	Go quickly and take this message.
An **exclamation** shows strong feeling.	One sun is hot enough!
• A **question** asks something. You can *answer* some questions with *yes* or *no*. • Other questions ask for more information. They begin with question words.	**Do** you like myths? Yes. **Is** this myth from Mexico? No. It's from China. **When? What? Why?** **Who? Where? How?**

Read Sentences

Read the passage. What kinds of sentences can you find? What question words do you see? Work with a partner.

The great emperor Shun cried out to Di Jun. "Why are you punishing us?" Shun's cries woke Di Jun and Xi He. They called to their sons. "Come back at once!"

Write Sentences

Look at the illustration on pages 94–95. Write two sentences about what Hou Yi is doing. Include one question. Compare your sentences with a partner's.

Language Frames

- _____ said _____ .
- We will check _____ .
- But _____ .

Verify

Listen to the song. Then use **Language Frames** to verify information of your own.

Song 🔊 ♪

Solar City

We'll build a solar city,
That's powered by the sun.
We will check our progress,
Until our goal is won.

Solutions to pollution,
That is our final aim.
They said we couldn't do it,
But look at what we've gained!

Tune: "This World Is What We Make It"

Key Words

Look at the diagram. Use **Key Words** to talk about how **solar** electricity works.

Key Words

circuit
conduct
current
electrical
insulate
solar
volt
watt

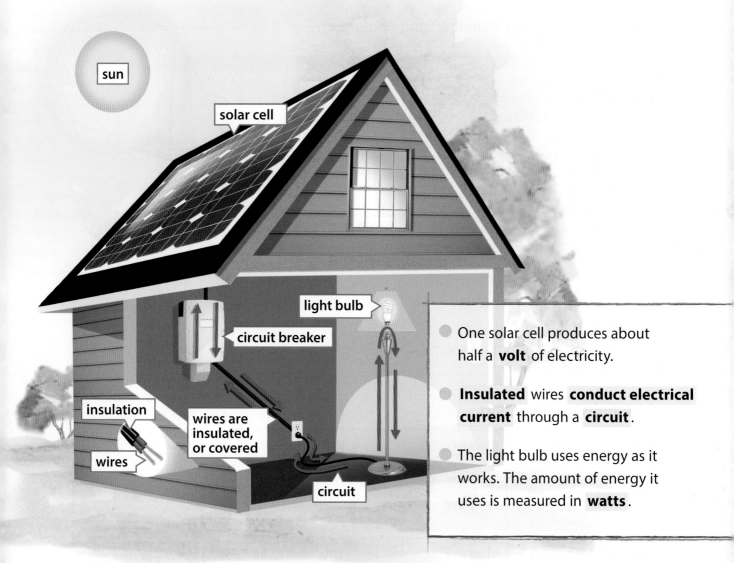

sun

solar cell

light bulb

circuit breaker

insulation

wires are insulated, or covered

wires

circuit

- One solar cell produces about half a **volt** of electricity.

- **Insulated** wires **conduct electrical current** through a **circuit**.

- The light bulb uses energy as it works. The amount of energy it uses is measured in **watts**.

Talk Together

How do we capture the sun's power? Talk with a partner. Use **Language Frames** from page 112 and **Key Words** to verify how people use solar energy.

Goal and Outcome

When you start a project, first you think about a **goal**, or what you want to happen. Sometimes during the project, you encounter problems, or obstacles. Then you use strategies to fix the problems. The **outcome** is the final result of the project.

Look at these pictures from the song "Solar City."

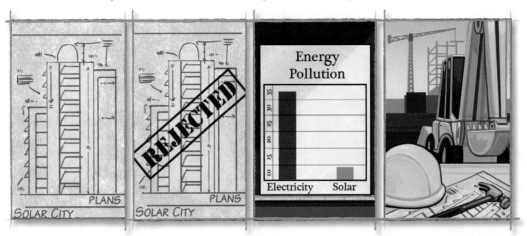

Map and Talk

You can use a goal-and-outcome chart to talk about a project. Here's how you make one.

Goal-and-Outcome Chart

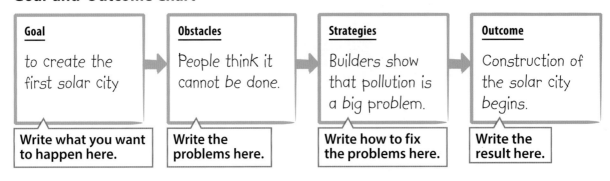

Goal	Obstacles	Strategies	Outcome
to create the first solar city	People think it cannot be done.	Builders show that pollution is a big problem.	Construction of the solar city begins.
Write what you want to happen here.	Write the problems here.	Write how to fix the problems here.	Write the result here.

Talk Together

With a partner, think of a project in your school. Use a goal-and-outcome chart to show the possible goal, obstacles, strategies, and outcome.

🔊 More Key Words

Use these words to talk about "Energy for the Future" and "How to Make a Solar Oven."

alternate
adjective

Alternate means different. He must find an **alternate** location.

decrease
verb

To **decrease** means to become less or smaller. When I spend money, my savings **decrease**.

energy
noun

Energy is the power to do work. It takes a lot of **energy** to run a marathon.

obstacle
noun

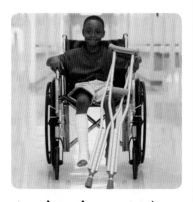

An **obstacle** is something that stops you from succeeding. A broken leg is an **obstacle** to riding a bike.

rely
verb

If you **rely** on something, you need it. We **rely** on electricity in our home.

Talk Together

With a partner, make an Expanded Meaning Map for each **Key Word**.

Expanded Meaning Map

Definition	Characteristics
source of power	powerful strong
Examples	**Non-examples**
electricity sunlight	rock pencil

energy

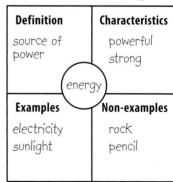

Learn to Ask Questions

Look at the diagram. Sometimes when you see an image, you **ask questions** about it. You may have to look again or look more carefully to find the answers.

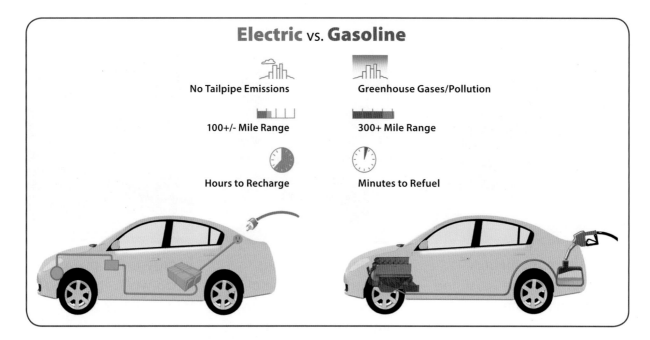

When you read, you can **ask questions**, too. The answers to some questions are **in your head**. Think to come up with answers. This will help you understand the text better.

How to Ask Questions

?	**1.** As you read, ask yourself a question.	I wonder _____ .
☁	**2.** Think about your experiences and what you know.	I think/Know _____ .
📖	**3.** Think about the answer. Read on and ask more questions.	Now I wonder _____ .

Talk Together

Read the blog. Read the sample. Use **Language Frames** to ask questions. Tell a partner about them.

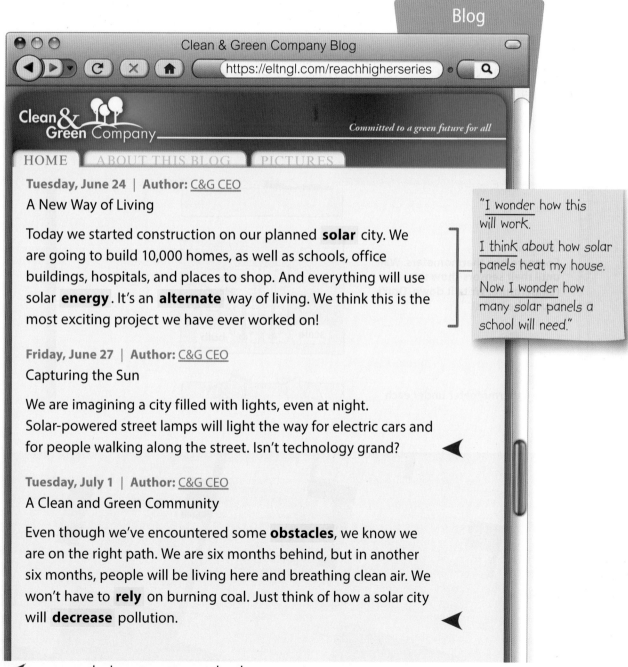

Blog

Clean & Green Company Blog

https://eltngl.com/reachhigherseries

Clean & Green Company   *Committed to a green future for all*

HOME   ABOUT THIS BLOG   PICTURES

Tuesday, June 24 | Author: C&G CEO

A New Way of Living

Today we started construction on our planned **solar** city. We are going to build 10,000 homes, as well as schools, office buildings, hospitals, and places to shop. And everything will use solar **energy**. It's an **alternate** way of living. We think this is the most exciting project we have ever worked on!

> "I wonder how this will work.
>
> I think about how solar panels heat my house.
>
> Now I wonder how many solar panels a school will need."

Friday, June 27 | Author: C&G CEO

Capturing the Sun

We are imagining a city filled with lights, even at night. Solar-powered street lamps will light the way for electric cars and for people walking along the street. Isn't technology grand? ◄

Tuesday, July 1 | Author: C&G CEO

A Clean and Green Community

Even though we've encountered some **obstacles**, we know we are on the right path. We are six months behind, but in another six months, people will be living here and breathing clean air. We won't have to **rely** on burning coal. Just think of how a solar city will **decrease** pollution. ◄

◄ = a good place to stop and ask a question

117

Read a Blog

Genre

A **blog** is a site on the Internet where someone posts his or her writing. Blog entries, or *posts*, usually appear in time order. In the past, people called such sites *web logs*. The name was later shortened to *blogs*.

Text Feature

A **diagram** shows the parts of something or how something works. A diagram often includes descriptive labels and may help illustrate a step in a process.

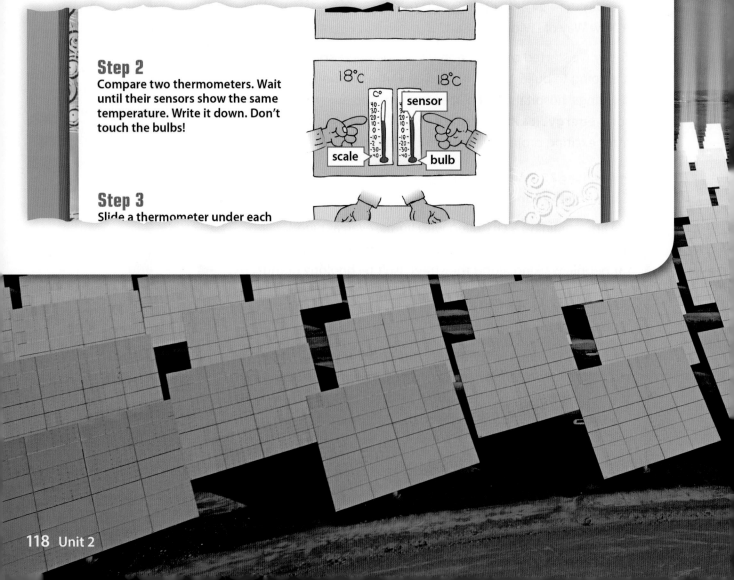

Step 2
Compare two thermometers. Wait until their sensors show the same temperature. Write it down. Don't touch the bulbs!

Step 3
Slide a thermometer under each

ENERGY
for the
FUTURE

by **Thomas Taha Rassam Culhane**

Solar C³ITIES Blog

https://eltngl.com/reachhigherseries

Solar C³ITIES

HOME | BLOG | ABOUT THIS BLOG | PICTURES | CREATE A BLOG

GREETINGS!

You have reached the **Solar** C³ITIES blog. Wait! Don't **click away**. If you want information about solar energy, you came to the right place.

First, let me introduce myself. I am Thomas Culhane, co-founder of Solar C³ITIES. My organization teaches about the most important source of energy in the world. Can you guess what it is? Hint: It's large, round, and fiery.

▲ **My goal is to teach people how they can use the sun's energy.**

It's the sun! The sun's energy is all around us, yet few people really **take advantage of** its power. My goal is to change that. I want to show people around the world how easy it is to **capture** the sun's energy for themselves. Click here or on the BLOG menu above to find out what Solar C³ITIES is **up to** lately.

click away leave this Web site
take advantage of make good use of
capture use
up to doing

HOME | BLOG | ABOUT THIS BLOG | PICTURES | CREATE A BLOG

Category: <u>Cairo, Egypt</u> | Date: Monday, April 5, 2010

Welcome to the City of the Sun

This week I am in Cairo, Egypt. I am here to teach a group of students how to use the sun's **energy** to heat water for their school. At our first meeting, I held up a large black **panel**. "We'll use something like this to heat the water," I told them. The students were confused. "Where is the **flame**?" they asked.

Over the next two weeks, the students will learn that to create heat energy, they don't always need a flame. In fact, they will become energy experts. I will post our lessons on this blog, along with updates on our progress. Our goal is to have their **solar** water heater **in place** by April 16th.

▲ I tell the kids they are going to become energy experts.

▲ Cairo was known by ancient Egyptians as "The City of the Sun."

POSTED BY: Thomas Culhane

2 COMMENTS   LINKS TO THIS POST

Search All Posts

BLOG ARCHIVE
January
Februray
March

POSTS BY CATEGORY
Cairo, Egypt
What Is Energy?
Chemical Energy
Electrical Energy
Light Energy
Thermal Energy
Putting It Together
Finding Solutions
We Did It!

April						
S	M	T	W	T	F	S
				1	2	3
4	5	6	7	8	9	10
11	12	13	14	15	16	17
18	19	20	21	22	23	24
25	26	27	28	29	30	

‹‹March

panel board
flame fire
in place ready to use

▶ **Before You Continue**

1. **Goal/Outcome** What two goals are stated in the blog?
2. **Analyze** Look at the headings and images. Does this blog seem informal? Why or why not?

121

What Is Energy?

Today I gave the students their first lesson in **energy** . I explained that energy is the ability to do work. Work isn't just what students do to get good grades, however. In science, work is what causes objects to move and change—including **human objects**. So when you move your body, even a little, you're doing work.

You don't have to be alive to do work, however. Objects can do work, too. Say you put some soup in the microwave. As soon as you press *On*, the **microwave** heats the soup. That change in temperature takes work.

All work requires energy. Luckily, energy comes in many different forms, and it can even change forms.

▲ **Everybody in this picture is using energy to do work.**

human objects people
microwave oven

Chemical Energy

One form of **energy** is chemical energy. You can find lots of it at the grocery store. That's because food is a form of chemical energy. When you eat food, chemical **reactions** inside your body break it down, giving you the energy you need to move and grow.

▲ **Food, such as fruit, provides chemical energy.**

Batteries also contain chemical energy. They power everything from watches, to cameras, to cell phones. They can even store energy to be used at another time.

Chemical energy **fuels** cars, too. The chemical energy in gasoline is what allows most buses, trains, and cars to get you where you need to go.

▲ **Batteries like these power a variety of portable devices.**

POSTED BY: Thomas Culhane

2 COMMENTS   LINKS TO THIS POST

---

reactions responses; actions
Batteries Objects that store **energy**
fuels powers
portable movable

▶ **Before You Continue**

1. **Clarify** Reread the first paragraph on this page. How are chemical energy and work connected?
2. **Paraphrase** Use your own words to explain what energy is.

Electrical Energy

Today I told the students about something truly "**shocking**"—**electrical energy**. For many people in the world, electrical energy, or electricity, makes life a lot easier. It makes lights glow, computers hum, water hot, and turns bread into toast! Electrical energy does work for people, so they can use their own energy for other things.

Most of the electrical energy in the world comes from power plants. A power plant is a place where machines called generators **transform** other forms of energy into electrical energy. Most power plants in the world get their energy from some form of chemical energy, like coal, oil, or natural gas.

▲ **The electricity you use probably comes from an electrical power plant like this one.**

shocking both amazing and charged with electricity

transform change

Have you ever boiled water on a stove? If so, then you understand how a fuel-based power plant works. Inside, burning fuel heats a large pool of water. At 100°**C** (212°**F**), the water boils, and steam rises from it. The **energy** contained in the steam turns a giant magnet surrounded by a **coil**. When the magnet spins, tiny, invisible **particles** inside the coil start to move. These particles are called electrons. Their movement creates **electrical** energy that flows through wires on poles to homes, businesses, and anywhere people need to plug something in.

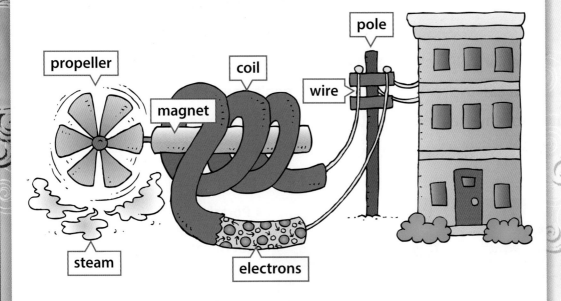

▲ **In a power plant, steam turns a magnet to produce electricity.**

POSTED BY: Thomas Culhane

7 COMMENTS   LINKS TO THIS POST

°**C** degrees Celsius
°**F** degrees Farenheit
coil large piece of wire wrapped into a roll
particles bits; pieces

▶ **Before You Continue**

1. **Ask Questions** What questions about power plants does the blog answer? What other questions do you have?

2. **Use Text Features** What is inside the coil wrapped around the magnet? What does the coil connect to?

Light Energy

I came to class today carrying my electric guitar. "Today I am going to teach you about my favorite form of **energy**," I told the students. "Light!"

What does an electric guitar have to do with light energy, you ask?

solar cells

solar panels

▲ **Solar cells turn light energy into electrical energy for my guitar.**

Well, thanks to **solar** cell technology, we can now use light energy directly, to create electricity. That means that I don't need to plug in to **an outlet** to play the electric guitar. I can just point my cells at the sun, plug in my guitar, and make beautiful music.

◀ **Portable solar panels let me plug in my guitar wherever there is sunlight. That means I can play musical chairs outdoors.**

an outlet place in the wall where you put a plug

Here is how **solar** cells work. You know that moving electrons create electricity. These electrons are held by larger particles, called atoms. Everything on Earth is made of atoms, and all atoms carry electrons. But some atoms are different than others. The atoms inside a solar cell, for example, are made to hold their electrons very loosely. When sunlight hits the cell, the atoms release their electrons easily. The freed electrons have electricity. That electricity goes by wire into a battery, or directly to a **circuit**.

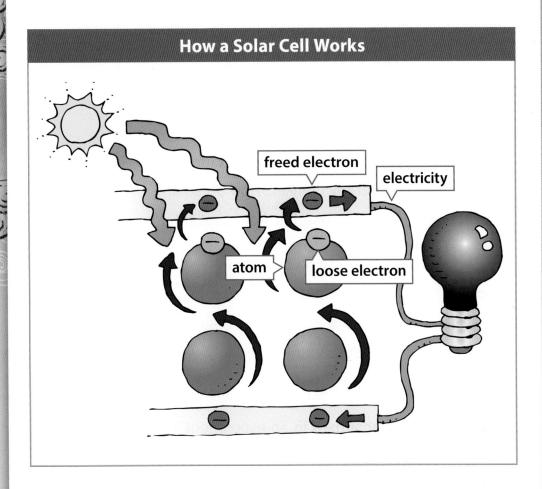

How a Solar Cell Works

POSTED BY: Thomas Culhane

4 COMMENTS   LINKS TO THIS POST

▶ **Before You Continue**

1. **Ask Questions** What question could you ask the author about **solar** cells?
2. **Analyze** How does the informal tone of this blog help you understand the information better?

Thermal Energy

I'm happy to say that **solar** cell technology is improving all the time. Soon, people may not have to **rely** on **distant** power plants for their **electrical** **energy**. But solar cells are still **relatively** **expensive**. There's an even easier way for people to use the power of the sun, and it's free!

Solar-powered water heaters use the sun's energy directly, without any special materials or technology. They take advantage of another important form of energy—thermal energy, or the energy of heat.

Thermal energy is all around us. Today, my students and I felt it in the warm air. Tonight, I feel it under my blanket. How do solar-powered water heaters capture it? They absorb it from sunlight.

The sun's light **produces** both visible light and heat energy. When light hits an object, its heat energy may be reflected or absorbed. If it is completely reflected, the heat energy bounces back into space. If it is completely absorbed, however, its heat energy stays. And it can make things very hot!

Today, the students and I became **absorbed in** an experiment that tests heat absorption. Try it and see the power of absorption for yourself.

distant faraway
relatively expensive more expensive than other power sources
produces makes
absorbed in very interested in

Reflection and Absorption: An Experiment

Step 1
Place one black and one white piece of paper in the sun.

Step 2
Compare two thermometers. Wait until their sensors show the same temperature. Write it down. Don't touch the bulbs!

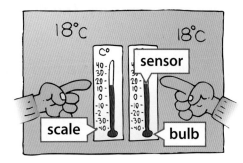

Step 3
Slide a thermometer under each piece of paper. Leave them in the sun for an hour.

Step 4
Compare the thermometers. Have the temperatures changed? Why?

POSTED BY: Thomas Culhane

5 COMMENTS   LINKS TO THIS POST

▶ **Before You Continue**

1. **Interpret** What do the results of the experiment show about the color black?
2. **Use Text Features** How do the sensor and scale work together to show the temperature?

129

Today, I held up the same black panel that I showed the students at our first meeting. This time, they knew exactly what it was for. "To absorb the sun's thermal **energy**!" they shouted.

The students and I will use our **knowledge** of heat and light energy as we build our water heater. The heater will contain water pipes lined with black aluminum fins. The fins will absorb the sun's heat energy and transfer it to the water in the pipes. As the water gets warmer, it will rise and move through the pipes into a storage **tank**.

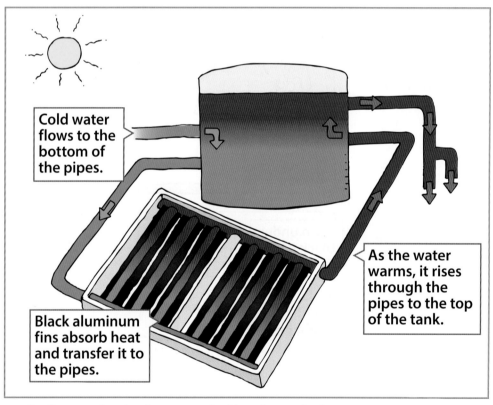

Cold water flows to the bottom of the pipes.

Black aluminum fins absorb heat and transfer it to the pipes.

As the water warms, it rises through the pipes to the top of the tank.

▲ As the sun heats the water, it rises through the pipes and into a storage tank.

knowledge understanding
tank container

Our first task is to build another **solar** panel. Solar panels are large, thin boxes with glass lids. They can be made out of **aluminum**, plastic, wood, or any other material you can shape into a box. The students and I will build our panel using aluminum. We're lucky because aluminum is **light** and easy to carry to a rooftop!

Next, we will **line** the box with **insulation**, and place our water pipes inside. The students know that the last step is also the most important: paint. The color black absorbs the most heat. So to make sure the pipes get really hot, we need to paint them, and their aluminum fins, black.

▲ **Solar panels are easy to make.**

▲ **Water pipes can be made of any common metal. Ours are made of copper.**

▲ **With a little black paint, the solar panel is finished.**

POSTED BY: Thomas Culhane

8 COMMENTS   LINKS TO THIS POST

aluminum metal
light not heavy
line cover the inside of

▶ **Before You Continue**

1. **Goal/Outcome** What actions are the students taking to reach their goal?
2. **Ask Questions** What questions could you ask the author about how the water heater will work?

Today we had a problem. We tested our metal storage tank. It leaked! Then one student had an idea. He took me to a place where plastic barrels from a shampoo factory were being resold. The barrels were **inexpensive** and perfect for our hot water heaters.

▲ **We have found a perfect hot water tank.**

When we returned, the students cheered. "But how will the water in the tank stay hot?" asked one student. "Maybe it just needs a blanket," said another.

▲ **With insulation, the water tank will not lose its heat as fast.**

Clearly, the students have become **energy** problem-solvers. At the end of the day today, we **insulated** our tank with a "blanket" of **fiberglass insulation** and then gave each other high-fives.

POSTED BY: Thomas Culhane

9 COMMENTS   LINKS TO THIS POST

inexpensive not high-priced
fiberglass insulation cloth made from glass

Today we finally reached our goal. The students cheered as I carefully placed the tank on a stand above the **solar** panels and filled it with cold water. We waited for most of the day as the cold water made its way through the pipes inside the panels. At the end of the day, we opened the pipe that carries hot water down to the schoolyard.

▲ **Pipes inside our solar panels heat the water.**

It worked! Hot water flowed from the pipe. It was even hot enough for a shower. The students were amazed at how easy it was to use the sun's **energy** . "This is just the beginning," I told them. "The real power is what you have learned about energy. One day, your knowledge will help you change the world!" ❖

POSTED BY: Thomas Culhane

▲ **The hot water is stored in our tank.**

▲ **The water is hot enough for a shower!**

14 COMMENTS   LINKS TO THIS POST

NEWER POSTS »

▶ **Before You Continue**

1. **Goal/Outcome** What two **obstacles** did Culhane and the students face on Thursday?

2. **Explain** How are the students **energy** problem-solvers?

Talk About It

1. What kind of information does Thomas Culhane post on his **blog**? Give two specific examples.

2. Imagine that you and a partner are writing a report on **solar** technology. You need to collect facts and **verify** them. Talk to your partner about what you know from this blog and what you need to verify. Use your own words.

   According to Mr. Culhane, solar technology _____ . I will check _____ to verify that _____ .

3. Think about the four types of **energy** discussed in this **blog**. Explain one of them and how you **rely** on it in your own life.

Write About It

A person who writes a **blog** often invites readers to ask questions. Write three questions about **solar energy** that you would like to post on Thomas Culhane's blog. Use **Key Words** and questions that start with *how, why, where.*

Why _____ ?
How _____ ?
Where _____ ?

Goal and Outcome

Make a goal-and-outcome chart to talk about what happened in
"Energy for the Future."

Goal-and-Outcome Chart

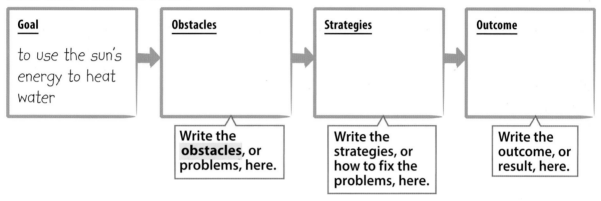

Goal	Obstacles	Strategies	Outcome
to use the sun's energy to heat water	Write the **obstacles**, or problems, here.	Write the strategies, or how to fix the problems, here.	Write the outcome, or result, here.

Now, use the chart to retell the selection
to a partner. Use **Key Words**. Record
your retelling.

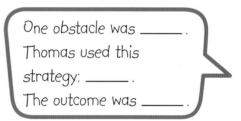

One obstacle was _____ .
Thomas used this
strategy: _____ .
The outcome was _____ .

Fluency

Practice reading with phrasing. Rate your reading.

Talk Together

Work together as a class. Describe how Thomas Culhane captures
sunlight to heat water. Have one student draw a diagram on the
board. Use **Key Words** as labels.

More Word Origins

Many English words contain a **root** that came from another language. Knowing the meaning of a word's root can help you determine the meaning of the word.

This chart shows some common roots.

Root	Origin	Meaning	Example
meter	Greek	measure	thermo**meter** , speedo**meter**
port	Latin	carry	re**port** , trans**port**
tru	Old English	faithful	**tru**e, **tru**th, **tru**thful

The Old English root *tru* means *faithful*. What do you think the word *truly* means?

Try It Together

Read the paragraph. Then answer the questions. Use the chart to help you.

> Solar panels can be made from plastic, wood, or aluminum. Some people use aluminum because it is <u>portable</u> and not heavy. When you make a solar panel, be sure the <u>perimeter</u> of the glass lid will fit the perimeter of the box.

1. Look for the Latin root in the word *portable*. What do you think **portable** means?

   A furniture

   B able to carry

   C a type of table

   D parts of a whole

2. Look for the Greek root *meter*. What do you think **perimeter** means?

   A wooden box

   B huge and heavy

   C measurement around

   D light and breakable

**NATIONAL
GEOGRAPHIC
EXCLUSIVE**

Making Connections Find out how the sun's **energy** can be used to heat food.

Genre A **how-to article** is a procedural text that gives instructions on how to do something. It may be in print or online. How-to articles are often written by an author or a contributor, who is an expert in the subject.

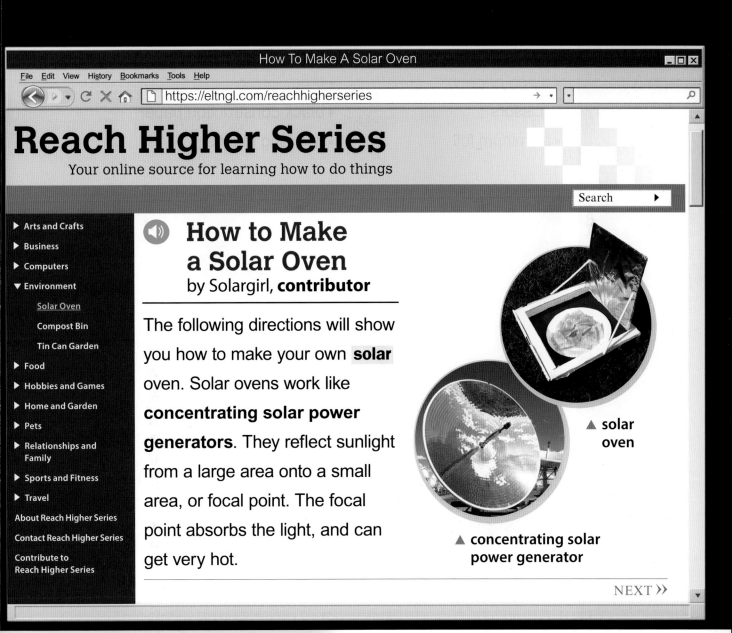

How To Make A Solar Oven

File Edit View History Bookmarks Tools Help

https://eltngl.com/reachhigherseries

Reach Higher Series
Your online source for learning how to do things

Search ▶

- ▶ Arts and Crafts
- ▶ Business
- ▶ Computers
- ▼ Environment
  - Solar Oven
  - Compost Bin
  - Tin Can Garden
- ▶ Food
- ▶ Hobbies and Games
- ▶ Home and Garden
- ▶ Pets
- ▶ Relationships and Family
- ▶ Sports and Fitness
- ▶ Travel

About Reach Higher Series

Contact Reach Higher Series

Contribute to
Reach Higher Series

How to Make a Solar Oven
by Solargirl, **contributor**

The following directions will show you how to make your own **solar** oven. Solar ovens work like **concentrating solar power generators**. They reflect sunlight from a large area onto a small area, or focal point. The focal point absorbs the light, and can get very hot.

▲ solar oven

▲ concentrating solar power generator

NEXT »

contributor person who writes the article for free

concentrating solar power generators machines that focus sunlight to make power

▶ **Before You Continue**

1. **Use Text Features** Compare the pictures. How is light reflected into the oven and onto the generator?

2. **Analyze** What makes this how-to article formal?

File   Edit   View   History   Bookmarks   Tools   Help

https://eltngl.com/reachhigherseries

Reach Higher Series
Your online source for learning how to do things

Search ▶

- ▶ Arts and Crafts
- ▶ Business
- ▶ Computers
- ▼ Environment
  - Solar Oven
  - Compost Bin
  - Tin Can Garden
- ▶ Food
- ▶ Hobbies and Games
- ▶ Home and Garden
- ▶ Pets
- ▶ Relationships and Family
- ▶ Sports and Fitness
- ▶ Travel

About Reach Higher Series

Contact Reach Higher Series

Contribute to Reach Higher Series

Things You Will Need

To make your **solar** oven, you will need these tools and materials:

- one large pizza box
- a pen or pencil
- scissors
- aluminum foil

- clear plastic wrap
- tape
- black construction paper
- two long straws

 Follow instructions carefully. Use materials and oven as instructed in the article.

Steps You Will Take

To make your **solar** oven, follow these steps:

Step **1**

Draw a square on the lid of a pizza box. The square should measure about one inch from all four sides of the lid.

Step **2**

Cut the square's sides and front. Do not cut the back edge of the square.

Step **3**

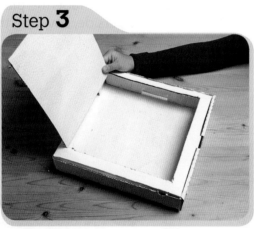

Fold up along the uncut line to form a flap. This is your oven's "solar **panel**."

« PREVIOUS | NEXT »

panel energy collector

▶ **Before You Continue**

1. **Make Inferences** What do you think is the purpose of the oven's "**solar** panel"?
2. **Steps in a Process** Which tools and materials do you use in the first three steps? What will you use next?

Reach Higher Series
Your online source for learning how to do things

Search ▶

Step **4**

Cut a piece of aluminum foil to fit the underside of the flap. Tape it in place. The foil will help reflect the sun's light into the box.

Step **5**

Cut a piece of clear plastic wrap slightly bigger than the flap. Open the flap. Tape the plastic to the lid's underside, covering the opening.

Step **6**

Tape a square of aluminum foil to the inside bottom of the box. This will help **insulate** it. Tape black construction paper over the foil. The paper will absorb the sun's thermal **energy**.

Step 7

Place food on the construction paper. **Solar** ovens work best for cooking things like nachos* at low temperatures. Close the lid and prop open the flap with straws. Tape the straws in place.

Step 8

Turn the oven toward the sun. Depending on the sun's **intensity**, your oven could reach 65°C (150°F) or more. Leave your oven in the sun until your food is warm.

Step 9

Solargirl's Cook Test Comparisons Table

Food	Solar Oven on a 30°C (86°F) Day	Regular Oven at 150°C (300°F)
nachos	cheese melted in 1 hour	cheese melted in 12 minutes
soup	turned warm but did not boil	boiled in 3 minutes
marshmallow	melted in 15 minutes	melted in 1 minute

* Tell a teacher or other adult before using a solar oven.

While your food is heating, think about how you can improve the design of your oven. Is there a better way to concentrate the sun's **energy** onto your box? Can you **insulate** it better? Finally, sit down and enjoy your food. You've **earned** it! ❖

Note: Solar ovens should only be used to heat up food that has already been cooked, such as nachos. Solar ovens should not be used to heat meat or eggs.

« PREVIOUS

intensity strength
earned worked hard for

▶ **Before You Continue**

1. **Paraphrase** In your own words, explain the last six steps in order.
2. **Use Text Features** What can you conclude about **solar** ovens, based on Solargirl's cook test comparisons?

Key Words	
alternate	insulate
circuit	obstacle
conduct	rely
current	solar
decrease	volt
electrical	watt
energy	

Compare Online Documents

You read two **online documents**. How are they alike? How are they different? Work with a partner to analyze and compare the online documents.

Comparison Chart

	"How to Make a Solar Oven"	"Energy for the Future"
Genre		
Point of View	Choose one: • first person • second person • third person	Choose one: • first person • second person • third person
Formal or Informal Did the writer use: • slang • exclamation points • abbreviations • questions • conversational voice	Choose one: • formal • informal	Choose one: • formal • informal

Analyze the writing. If the writer used three or more of these writing styles, then the writing is informal.

Talk Together

Think about the two selections and the chart above. Use these resources and **Key Words** to discuss how people can use the sun's power.

Compound and Complex Sentences

A **compound sentence** has two independent clauses, or sentences. A **complex sentence** has an independent clause and a dependent clause.

Grammar Rules	Compound and Complex Sentences
For **compound sentences:** Use a <u>comma</u> plus a <u>conjunction</u> to join two independent clauses.	Plants use light energy, **and** people rely on it. The sun's energy is all around us, **but** few people take advantage of it. Machines can run on electrical energy, **or** they can use solar energy.
For **complex sentences:** If the **dependent clause** comes first, put a <u>comma</u> after it. Do not use a comma if the **independent clause** comes first.	**Since the beginning of time,** the sun has been a powerful force. **The sun has been a powerful force** since the beginning of time.

Read Compound and Complex Sentences

Read the passage. What compound and complex sentences can you find?

> We feel heat on a hot day because thermal energy is all around us. It comes from the movement of atoms. When they move quickly, they give off heat.

Write Compound and Complex Sentences

Write one compound sentence and one complex sentence describing light energy. Compare your sentences with the sentences of a partner.

Write As a Storyteller

Write a Myth

Write a myth that explains how something in nature came to be. You and your classmates will share your myths with a group of younger students.

Study a Model

A myth is a story that explains something about the world. It usually has gods or other non-human beings that act in human ways. Read Ted's myth about why there are earthquakes.

The story begins by introducing the **characters**.

What Makes the Earth Quake?
by Ted Walzcak

Before there were people in the world, there were **giants**. They were the ones who cared for the Earth. They planted forests. They built mountains. They made places for rivers to flow.

After a few thousand years, **some of the giants got pretty tired** of working. They wanted to have fun! So they started ripping up the trees and knocking down mountains. They even blocked rivers to make the land flood!

The writer describes the **conflict**, or problem.

The writer uses **different kinds of sentences** to make the story interesting.

The gods were upset. What could they do? Finally, they decided to put the troublemakers in big caves deep inside the earth. That would stop the mischief!

Well, the trapped giants weren't very happy. When they pound on the walls of their caves, the ground above shakes and cracks. That's why we have earthquakes!

Prewrite

1. Choose a Topic What event in nature could you use a myth to explain? Talk with a partner to choose an idea that would be fun to write about.

2. Gather Information What will happen in your story? Write down the details you will use to develop the characters and events.

3. Get Organized Use a chart to help you organize your details.

Character Chart

Character	Role	Function	Conflict
giants			want to have fun by destroying things
gods			

Draft

Use your chart and details to write your draft.

• Your title should say what the myth will be about.

• In the first paragraph, introduce your characters and setting.

• Next, write what the conflict is and how the characters react.

Revise

1. **Read, Retell, Respond** Read your draft aloud to a partner. Your partner listens and then retells the myth. Next, talk about ways to improve your writing.

Language Frames

Retell	Make Suggestions
• Your myth explains _____ . • Your characters are _____ , and your setting is _____ . • First, _____ . Then, _____ . Finally, _____ .	• I couldn't picture your characters. You could add details about _____ . • I didn't understand why _____ .

> Use sentences like these to respond to your partner's writing.

---

2. **Make Changes** Think about your draft and your partner's suggestions. Then use revision marks to make your changes.

   • Do all your details help develop your idea? Remove any that don't.

   > Finally, they decided to put the troublemakers in big caves deep inside the Earth. ~~Each one was the size of Mammoth Cave! The gods figured~~ that would stop the mischief!

   • Different types of sentences will make your writing more interesting. Turn some simple sentences into compound and complex sentences.

   > When
   > They pound on the walls of their caves, The ground above shakes and cracks.

Edit and Proofread

Work with a partner to edit and proofread your myth. Make sure you've punctuated compound and complex sentences correctly. Also check that you have used the correct end mark for each sentence. Use revision marks to show your changes.

Punctuation Tip

In a compound sentence, add a comma before the conjunction that connects the two parts.

Present

On Your Own Make a final copy of your myth. Choose a way to share your work with your classmates. You can read it aloud, or act it out.

Presentation Tips	
If you are the speaker...	**If you are the listener...**
Make sure you change your tone to show questions and exclamations.	Listen for details that tell you what the writer is trying to explain or teach.
Make eye contact with your listeners to help them stay connected.	Smile or nod to show the speaker that you are enjoying the story.

In a Group Myths were usually passed on by storytellers. Arrange to visit a class of younger children and share your myths with them. Afterwards, ask them to draw pictures to go with your story. Later, you can post your myths on your school's Web site.

? BIG Question

What is the power of the sun?

Talk Together

In this unit, you found lots of answers to the **Big Question**. Now, use the concept map to discuss the **Big Question** with the class.

Concept Map

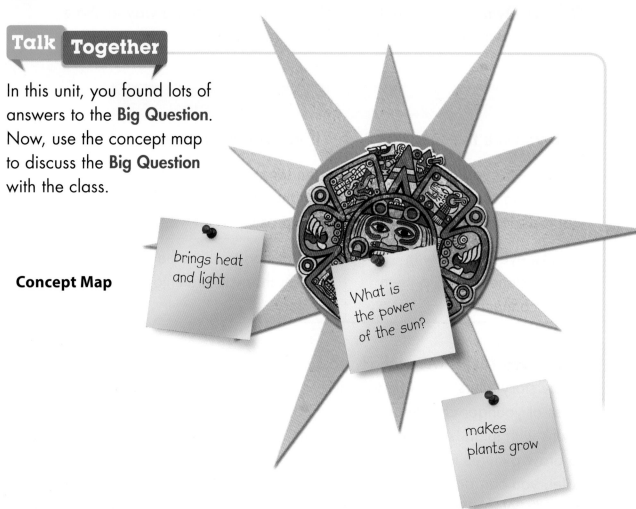

brings heat and light

What is the power of the sun?

makes plants grow

Write a Compare and Contrast Blog ✏️

Use the concept map to write a blog that explains how the power of the sun affects people and nature.

Share Your Ideas

Choose one of these ways to share your ideas about
the **Big Question**.

Write It!

Write to an Astronaut

Write a letter to an astronaut.
Include a question you would
like to ask about the Sun. Use the
Internet to search
the NASA Web
site for the
address where
you should send
the letter.

Dear NASA
Astronaut,
I heard that the
view of the Sun from
space is amazing!
I have a question
about the Sun.

Talk About It!

Hold a Press Conference

With a partner, hold a
"press conference" about the
first solar oven at your school.
First, prepare interesting facts
and details. Tell this information
to an audience of "reporters"
(your classmates). Then invite the
reporters to ask questions.

Do It!

Perform a Myth

Choose a myth from the unit.
Work with a group of classmates
to perform it as a play. Decide
who will play each part. Then talk
about how you will perform the
key events. Create some props and
costumes. Rehearse the play
several times and then
perform it for the class.

Write It!

Write a Song or Chant

Work with a partner to write a
song or chant to introduce one of
the selections. The song or chant
should match the mood or
feeling of the selection.
Perform the song
or chant for
the class.

Nature's Webs

? BIG Question

How are animals and plants dependent on one another?

AMAZONAS, BRAZIL
A frog catching a cricket with its tongue
in the Amazon rainforest

Unit at a Glance
▸ **Language Focus**: Tell an Original Story, Engage in Conversation
▸ **Reading Strategy**: Determine Importance
▸ **Topic**: Food Webs, Ecosystems

Share What You Know

❶ **Think** about what animals eat.

❷ **Draw** an animal on a note card and **label** it.

❸ **Tell** the class what plant or animal your animal eats.

Do It!

fish

Language Focus

- The story happens at/in _____ .
- The story is about _____ .
- The _____ problem is _____ .

Tell an Original Story

Listen to Melissa's song, which tells a story about a hawk and a squirrel.

The Hawk and the Squirrel

Song 🔊 ♪

The story happens out in my backyard,
Where lots of squirrels like to play.
One day, a big hawk comes to my backyard.
The story is about that day.

A baby squirrel is out in the open,
When I see a hawk outside.
The squirrel's problem is he is out there
With nowhere good for him to hide.

I see the hawk dive. I have to think fast.
The baby squirrel depends on me.
I make a big noise. The hawk is frightened.
The squirrel runs safely up a tree.

Tune: "La Cucaracha"

Key Words

Key Words

| carnivore |
| consumer |
| food chain |
| herbivore |
| omnivore |
| producer |

Look at the diagram. Use **Key Words** and other words to talk about the relationship between plants and animals in a **food chain**.

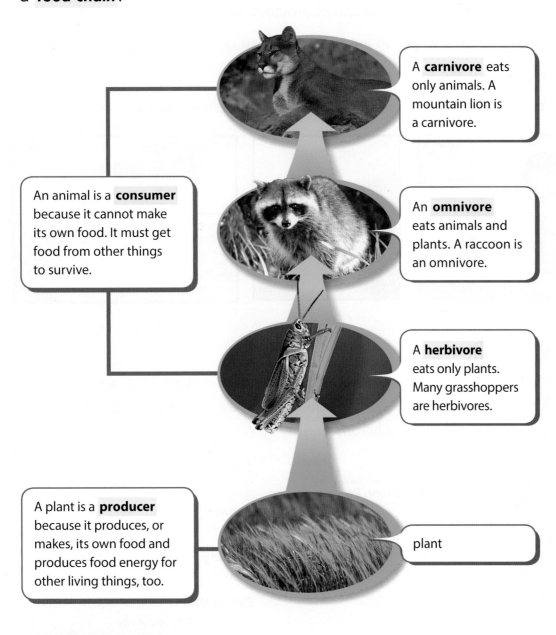

A **carnivore** eats only animals. A mountain lion is a carnivore.

An animal is a **consumer** because it cannot make its own food. It must get food from other things to survive.

An **omnivore** eats animals and plants. A raccoon is an omnivore.

A **herbivore** eats only plants. Many grasshoppers are herbivores.

A plant is a **producer** because it produces, or makes, its own food and produces food energy for other living things, too.

plant

Talk Together

How are living things in nature connected? With a partner, use the **Key Words** to answer this question.

Plot

Plot is what happens in a story. Plots are built around a problem that the main character faces.

- The events happen because of the characters' actions.
- The turning point is when an important change occurs.
- The resolution is the event that solves the problem.

Look at the pictures. They show what happens in Melissa's story.

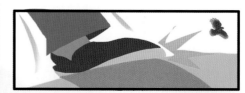

Map and Talk

You can use a plot diagram to keep track of parts in a story. First, say what the problem is. Then, tell the events in the order they happen. Next, tell the turning point. Last, tell the resolution.

Plot Diagram

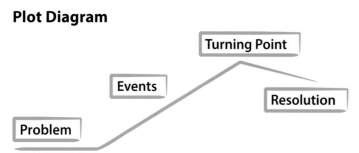

Problem: The baby squirrel is in danger from the hawk.

Events: The hawk flies down toward the baby squirrel. Melissa sees it.

Turning Point: When Melissa makes noise, the hawk flies away.

Resolution: The baby squirrel climbs up the tree to safety.

Work with your partner to retell an animal story you know or have experienced. Use a plot diagram to help you retell the story.

More Key Words

Use these words to talk about "Coyote and Badger" and "Living Links."

cooperate
verb

When you **cooperate**, you work together. We **cooperated** to clean up our messy room.

essential
adjective

Essential means important and necessary. Water is **essential** for our survival.

partnership
noun

Individuals in a **partnership** work together and share the results of their work.

store
verb

When you **store** something, you keep it somewhere until it is needed.

transfer
verb

Transfer means to move from one place to another. She **transfers** the food to the plate.

Talk Together

Make a Vocabulary Example Chart for each **Key Word**. Then compare your chart with a partner's.

Word	Definition	Example
store	Keep	old games in my closet

155

Learn to Determine Importance

To determine what's important, focus on what matters. One way to determine what's important is to **summarize**, or tell only the most important information.

Look for the most important details in the picture to help you summarize Melissa's day with her friends.

When you read, you can look for important details to help you **summarize**, too.

How to Summarize

?	**1.** Identify the topic. Ask, "What is the paragraph mostly about?"	The topic is _____ .
👁	**2.** Look for the important details.	Detail #1 is _____ . Detail #2 is _____ .
✏	**3.** Talk about the topic and the most important ideas.	The paragraph is about _____ .

Language Frames

? The topic is _____.

👁 Detail #1 is _____.
Detail #2 is _____.

✏ The paragraph
is about _____.

Read Melissa's personal narrative. Read the sample summary. Then use **Language Frames** to summarize the narrative to a partner.

Personal Narrative

The Oak Tree

My brother and I love to explore the woods behind my family's house. Lots of different plants and animals live there. My favorite place is the big oak tree. It is an **essential** place for the animals. It gives them food and a home. Red squirrels gather nuts from the tree and **store** them there for the winter. Birds build their nests in the oak tree.

Last week, there was a terrible storm. Lightning hit the oak tree, and it caught fire. By the time the fire was out, most of the tree was gone. The squirrels and birds lost their home, but we're happy that they weren't harmed in the fire. The squirrels lost their food, too. Without their winter supply of nuts, they were in real trouble.

We had to do something. My brother and I formed a **partnership** to help the squirrels. We gathered many nuts and seeds for them. Then we put them at the edge of the woods for the squirrels to find. The squirrels were able to **transfer** our nuts and seeds to their new home in another tree. When my brother and I **cooperate**, we can do anything!

"The topic is the oak tree in the woods.
Detail #1 is the oak tree provides food and a home for the squirrels.
Detail #2 is birds live in the oak tree.
The paragraph is about the importance of the oak tree."

◄ = a good place to stop and summarize

Read a Story

Genre

Realistic fiction is a story that sounds as if it could be true. The characters, plot, and setting seem real.

Setting

The setting of a story is where and when it takes place. This story takes place in Chaco Canyon, New Mexico. Long ago, a Native American community lived there. They built large clay buildings, called *pueblos*.

As you look at the pictures in "Coyote and Badger," try to find pueblos and other signs of ancient Native American culture.

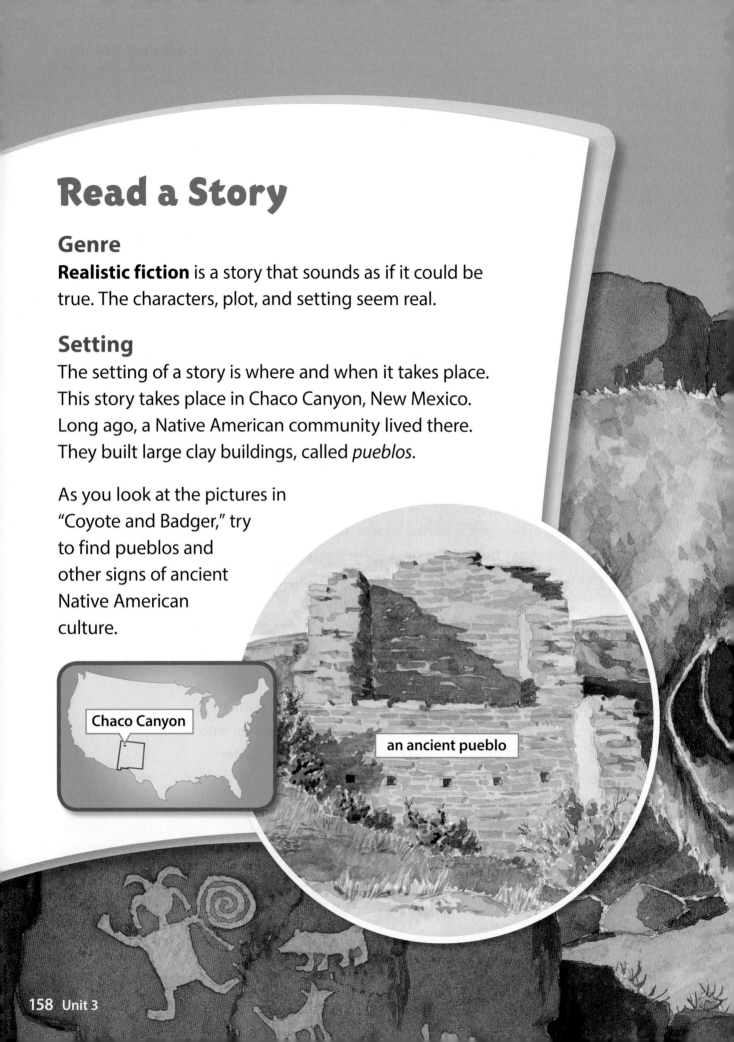

Chaco Canyon

an ancient pueblo

COYOTE AND BADGER

written and illustrated by
Bruce Hiscock

▶ **Set a Purpose**
The animals of Chaco Canyon
have a problem. What is it?

Coyote woke up hungry, again. He stretched and looked out at the desert. **The sun was going down**, but the air was still hot. Coyote hoped to **spy** a rabbit, or even a mouse, since he hadn't eaten in two days.

These were hard times for all the animals of Chaco Canyon. No rain had fallen that spring, and there were no fresh leaves for the small animals to feed on.

And so Coyote, the hunter, often went hungry, too. Now he trotted silently up the canyon to **try his luck** once more.

The sun was going down It was nearly night
spy find
try his luck try to find food

Across the **dry stream**, Coyote scared up a rabbit,
and a dizzy chase began. The rabbit **streaked** through the
saltbush, with Coyote snapping at its heels. For a moment,
it looked as though **Old Hunter** might eat well. But the
cottontail was too quick and squeezed between some
rocks by the canyon wall. Coyote scratched around
the hiding place awhile and then went to look for
something slower, or maybe something
dead, to eat.

dry stream creek without water
streaked ran quickly
Old Hunter Coyote
cottontail rabbit

Farther up the canyon, Badger **emerged from her den**.
She left her two pups safely underground and **waddled off** as the
air began to cool. Badger was a night hunter, too, but she **seldom
chased rabbits**. She was a digger, not a runner.

When Badger found the hole of an antelope squirrel, she
tore into the hard soil with her long claws. The dirt flew, and
in a wink, she was underground following a dark tunnel. No
animal can dig as fast as a badger, but the squirrel raced ahead
and escaped.

emerged from her den came out of her home
waddled off walked away
seldom chased rabbits didn't hunt rabbits often
tore into started digging with a lot of energy
in a wink soon

Badger dug many holes that night before she came home
with meat for the pups. **Prey was scarce** now, especially around
the den. It was time to move her family to a new hunting ground.

As the sun rose, Badger led the way down the canyon with
her little ones close behind. Few animals ever **messed with**
Badger, for she was a fierce fighter. But **the open desert** is a
dangerous place for pups. Overhead, in the clear morning air,
an eagle watched them closely.

Prey was scarce Food was hard to find
messed with tried to attack
the open desert land with no place to hide

▶ **Before You Continue**

1. **Plot** Why is the dry weather a problem for Coyote and Badger? How do you think it will affect them in the future?

2. **Make Inferences** Why is the eagle watching Badger and her pups so closely?

At last they reached one
of Badger's other **burrows** by
an old pueblo. She checked
the tunnel for rattlesnakes,
as the pups scurried into
their new home.

Not far from there,
Coyote settled down to sleep
for the day. He was still
terribly hungry.

When evening came,
Badger began hunting.
Coyote heard the sound
of her digging. Quietly,
carefully, he **stole** closer.

Suddenly a kangaroo rat, **fleeing** from
Badger, hopped from a tunnel. A quick **pounce**
and Coyote had food. Another rat, about to leave
its burrow, saw Coyote and fled back down the
tunnel. That rat became Badger's dinner.

burrows homes
stole moved
fleeing running
pounce attack

When Badger **scrambled** back to the surface, she found Coyote waiting. Instantly she backed away, showing her powerful teeth. For a moment the two animals faced each other, hissing, growling, their fur standing **on end**. Then a curious thing happened. As they sniffed each other's scent, they relaxed a little.

Coyote came forward. He **took in** Badger's musky odor, while she could almost smell the hunger on his fur. And as they circled one another, the ancient and mysterious bond between coyotes and badgers **took hold**.

scrambled climbed quickly
on end straight up
took in smelled
took hold returned

They began hunting together that very night. Coyote, the **swift** runner, led the way to a prairie dogs' den as Badger shuffled behind.

Then Badger, **the master** digger, went to work. With Coyote **standing guard**, there was no safe place for the prairie dogs above ground or below. Soon each partner had a full belly, and Badger was headed home, carrying meat for the pups.

In the nights that followed, Coyote and Badger became a **fearsome** team. Not every hunt was successful, but it was much better than hunting alone.

swift fast
the master who was a very good
standing guard watching and waiting
fearsome strong

▶ **Before You Continue**

1. **Plot** How do Coyote and Badger solve their problem? What do you think will happen in the future as a result?

2. **Summarize** Summarize the most important story events so far.

▶ **Predict**
Will Coyote and Badger keep
hunting together?

The **drought** grew worse as summer arrived. Each cactus, once **swollen with** water, **shrank** as it waited for the rains to begin.

Coyote and Badger often traveled far in search of prey, resting side by side when they grew tired. But they seldom went hungry, and Badger always took meat back to her pups.

The pups were getting big now. Badger let them play and dig little holes by the burrow when she was home. They were so full of energy and life.

drought dry weather
swollen with full of
shrank got smaller

Then one morning, Badger returned from a long hunt with Coyote to find only one pup in the den. She looked for the missing youngster at his favorite digging spot, but there was no sign of him. Badger searched everywhere. Then, behind the pueblo, she found **shreds** of fur, some blood, and an eagle feather. Badger, mother of many pups, knew this one would never return.

When Coyote looked for Badger that evening, she was gone. He found Badger's trail, but he did not follow it. **The time of parting had come**.

shreds pieces
The time of parting had come. It was time to hunt separately again.

169

Coyote went back to hunting by himself. Even mice were hard to find now, for the rains still had not come. Through the dark nights, Coyote searched for food, and **when the sun burned down**, he slept.

One night as Coyote **prowled** near **the ruins of an ancient kiva**, the Old Hunter threw back his head and let out a long yip and howl. From around the canyon, other coyotes joined in. The song echoed off the dark walls and floated up toward the river of stars in the sky.

when the sun burned down during the day
prowled hunted
the ruins of an ancient kiva an old Native
    American meeting room

Late the next afternoon, Coyote woke to the rumble of distant thunder. Wind rippled through the dry grass, and Coyote caught the **scent** of rain.

In her den, Badger felt a tingle as lightning **split** the sky. The summer rains were here at last. Now the desert would be green again, and for a time there would be more food for all the animals.

Badger listened as the rain **swept up** the canyon. And deep in the storm she heard something strange, yet familiar. It sounded like Coyote, howling in the wind.

---

scent smell
split flashed through the middle of
swept up moved quickly into

▸ **Before You Continue**

1. **Plot** What did Badger do after her pup was killed? Why do you think she did it?
2. **Explain** The phrase "caught the scent" is an idiom. What do you think it means?

PREDATOR PARTNERS

For hundreds of years, people have told stories about coyotes and badgers hunting together. In the mid-1980s, scientists saw this strange event many times in Wyoming's National Elk Refuge. When coyotes were hunting squirrels above ground, badgers looked for squirrels below ground, in burrows. Some coyotes would wait for the badgers to **flush out squirrels** from the burrows. If a coyote didn't catch a squirrel, sometimes the badger would get it.

Scientists found that coyotes who hunted with badgers caught more squirrels than those who hunted alone! ❖

Badgers like this one sometimes hunt with coyotes. ▼

flush out squirrels chase the squirrels out

Meet the Author and Illustrator

BRUCE HISCOCK

Bruce Hiscock loves to draw—and he believes that anyone can learn how. He says, "Practice is the only way to improve."

Bruce has been practicing for a long time. When he was a child, he spent a lot of time outdoors. When he grew up, he became a scientist, and then an author and illustrator.

Bruce has explored natural places in the United States and Canada. He always travels with a sketchbook and a journal. He visited Chaco Canyon three times while working on this book.

This is how Bruce draws a mouse. Follow his steps and draw your own. ▼

▲ Bruce Hiscock likes to spend time in his studio, where he works on his writing and drawing.

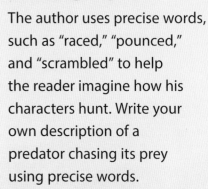

Writing Tip ✏️

The author uses precise words, such as "raced," "pounced," and "scrambled" to help the reader imagine how his characters hunt. Write your own description of a predator chasing its prey using precise words.

173

Talk About It

Key Words

carnivore	omnivore
consumer	partnership
cooperate	producer
essential	store
food chain	transfer
herbivore	

1. What seems **realistic** about this **fiction** story?

_____ could really happen in the desert.
Coyotes _____ in real life.
Badgers _____ in real life.

2. Imagine that Coyote and Badger meet again. **Tell an original story** about what they do.

The story happens in _____ .
The story is about _____ .
This time Coyote and Badger's problem is _____ .
This is how the characters solve the problem: _____ .

3. Think about the **partnership** Coyote and Badger have. What surprises you about it, based on what you know about these animals?

Write About It

Do you think the desert ecosystem is a difficult place for animals to survive? Write a paragraph. Use **Key Words** to explain why or why not.

I think the desert ecosystem _____ .
One reason is _____ .

Plot

Make a plot diagram for "Coyote and Badger."

Plot Diagram

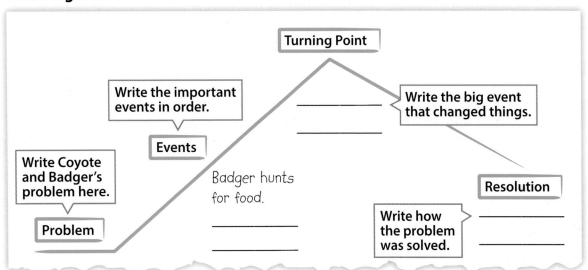

Turning Point

Write the important
events in order.

Write the big event
that changed things.

Events

Write Coyote
and Badger's
problem here.

Badger hunts
for food.

Resolution

Problem

Write how
the problem
was solved.

Now use your plot diagram as you retell
the story to a partner. Use **Key Words** in
your retelling.

> The problem is _____ .
> Coyote and Badger _____ .
> The turning point happens
> when _____ .

Fluency

Practice reading with intonation. Rate your reading.

The illustration on pages 166–167 shows how Coyote and Badger
work together. Use **Key Words** to tell a partner what the illustration
shows about how living things are connected.

Prefixes

Many long words begin with a **prefix**, or a short word part, like *dis-* and *un-*. Many of these English prefixes came from Latin, Greek, or Old English. Sometimes knowing the meaning of the prefix can help you predict the meaning of the word.

This chart shows some common prefixes.

Prefix	Origin	Meaning	Example
in-	Latin	not	indirect, incapable
micro-	Greek	small	microculture
mis-	Old English	wrongly	misuse, mistake

The prefix *mis-* means *wrongly*. What do you think the word *misjudge* means?

Try It Together

Read the sentences. Then answer the questions. Use the chart above to help you.

Some people have studied the microculture of coyotes and badgers and have evidence that they sometimes work together to find food. Others think this is inaccurate. They believe coyotes and badgers wouldn't work together since they are natural enemies.

1. **Look for the Greek prefix in the word *microculture*. What do you think microculture means?**

   A animal culture

   B life in forests

   C culture of small groups

   D behavior of large groups

2. **Look for the Latin prefix *in-*. What do you think inaccurate means?**

   A true

   B not accurate

   C wrongly support

   D the opposite of hungry

Living Links

Making Connections Learn another way that living things depend on each other to survive.

Genre **Expository nonfiction** is any text that gives facts and information about a topic.

by **Diane Salisian**

As the desert sun sets, a bat flies out of her cave. It's time for dinner. She lands on a nearby cactus and begins to dine on its fruit. Suddenly, an owl **snatches her**. It's time for the owl to eat, too!

The cactus, the bat, and the owl are parts, or links, in one desert food chain. In a food chain, each living thing transfers its energy to the living thing that eats it.

A Desert Food Chain

1. A saguaro cactus uses the sun's energy to make food.

2. The saguaro flower's pollen is food for the Mexican long-tongued bat.

3. The bat is food for the desert great horned owl.

Links Connections
snatches her takes her away

▶ **Before You Continue**

1. **Summarize** In your own words, explain how a **food chain** works, beginning with the sun.

2. **Use Text Features** How does a bat get energy and pass it along?

Desert Producers

Plants are an important link in any **food chain**. Through the process of photosynthesis, they take in energy from the sun and **transform** it into food. They use this food to grow roots, stems, leaves, and flowers.

Plants are like living **energy storage lockers**. When a plant is eaten, all the energy it contains comes out of storage. The plant then **transfers** that energy to the animal that eats it. That's why plants are called **producers**. They produce, or make, not only their own food, but also the food energy that other living things need for life.

Plants **store** another thing—water! The shape of these cacti helps them store as much water as possible.

transform change
energy storage lockers places that store energy

Desert Consumers

Consumers are everywhere in the desert. Just listen for their **chirps**, rattles, growls, and **squeals**. Consumers are the animals that call the desert home. Unlike **producers**, they cannot make their own food. They must eat other things in order to survive.

Consumers are grouped by the kind of food they eat. **Herbivores** are animals that eat plants. In the desert, they may nibble on seeds, flowers, roots, and grasses. Some herbivores get most of their water from the plants they eat.

Carnivores are animals that eat other animals. Eagles, snakes, and bobcats are desert carnivores. **Omnivores**, on the other hand, are not picky. They may eat any plant or animal that looks appetizing, including eggs, fruits, and insects. Consumers **form** another important link in any **food chain**.

herbivore

carnivore

omnivore

chirps quiet noises
squeals loud noises
form make

▶ **Before You Continue**

1. **Main Idea** How do **producers** get energy? How do **consumers** get energy?
2. **Analyze** How does the author organize her ideas? How does this organization help you understand the text?

179

Desert Decomposers

When a plant or an animal dies, the energy **stored** in its body does not go away. Instead, it is transformed once again. This time decomposers, such as fungi (including mushrooms) and bacteria, do the work.

Decomposers help break down dead plants and animals. As they dine, they return **essential nutrients** to the soil. Plants need these nutrients in order to survive.

◀ Bacteria are decomposers that live in the desert soil.

The sun, **producers**, **consumers**, and decomposers are all linked. In ecosystems like the desert, they form networks of **food chains**, called food webs. By studying food webs, we can better understand how all living things are connected. ❖

essential nutrients what plants need to grow

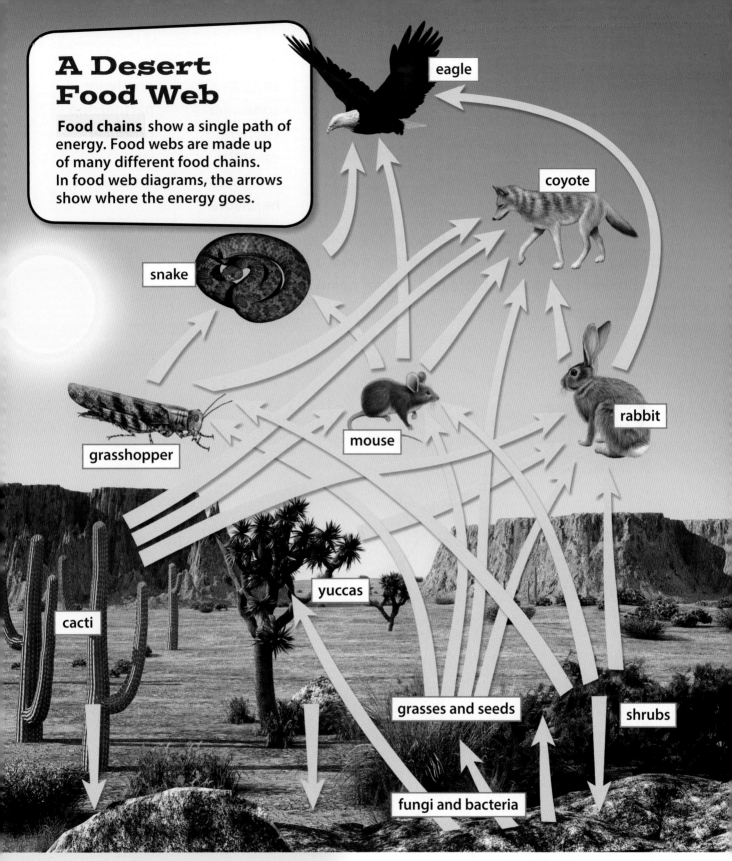

A Desert Food Web

Food chains show a single path of energy. Food webs are made up of many different food chains. In food web diagrams, the arrows show where the energy goes.

eagle

coyote

snake

rabbit

grasshopper

mouse

yuccas

cacti

grasses and seeds

shrubs

fungi and bacteria

▶ **Before You Continue**

1. **Details** What is the role of decomposers in an ecosystem?

2. **Use Text Features** Find one food chain in the food web diagram. Explain how energy flows through it.

Compare Content

In "Living Links," you learned how plants and animals are connected in a food web. Where do the plants and animals from "Coyote and Badger" belong in a food web? With a partner, make a food web like the one below. Write each plant and animal name where it fits in the web.

Food Web

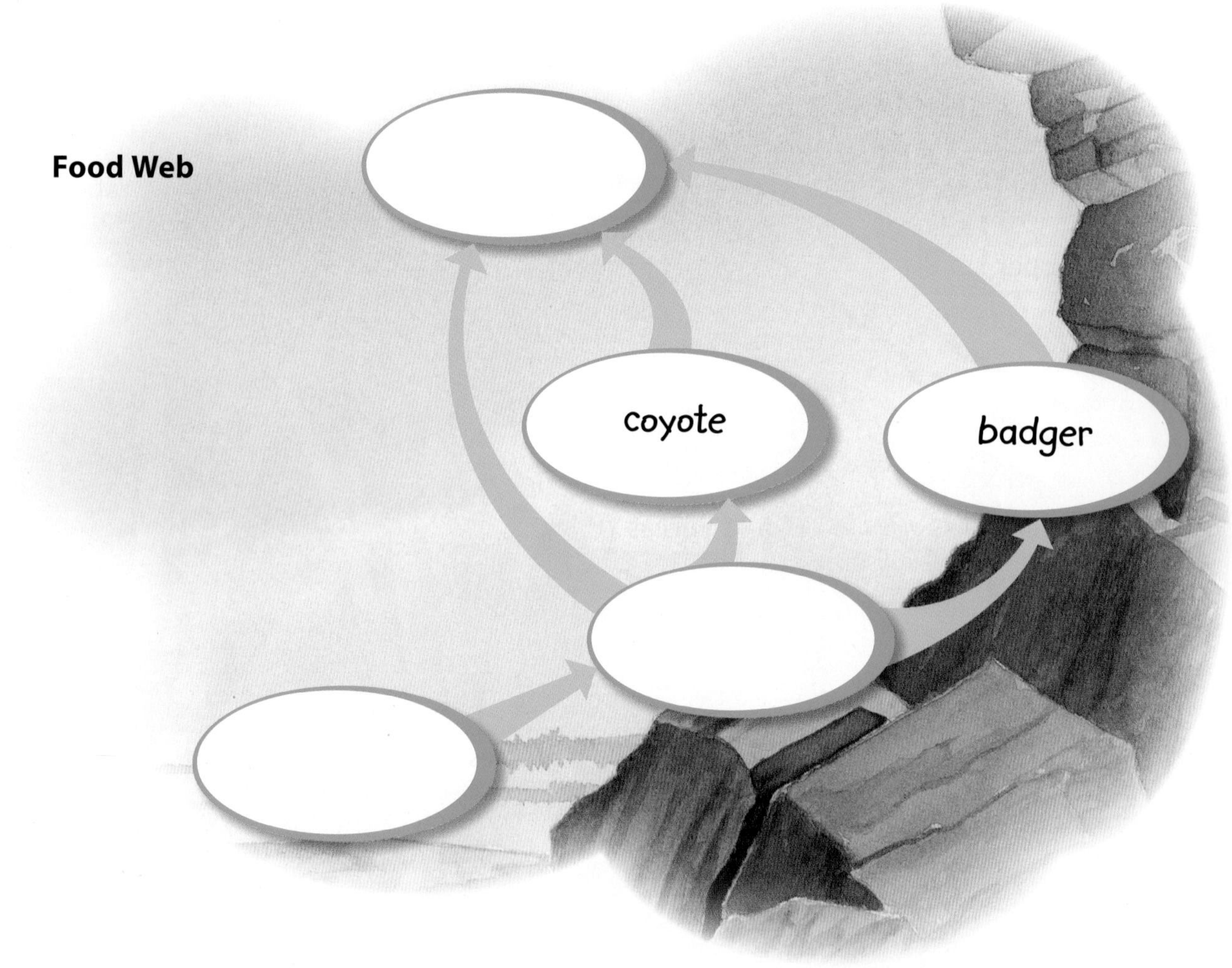

( ) coyote   ( ) badger

Talk Together

How are the animals and plants in this food web connected? Use **Key Words** to talk about your ideas.

Plural Nouns

A **noun** names a person, place, thing, or idea. A **singular noun** shows "one." A **plural noun** shows "more than one."

Grammar Rules — Plural Nouns

	singular nouns	plural nouns
• Add **–s** to most nouns to show more than one.	tunnel	tunnel**s**
• Add **–es** to nouns that end in **x**, **ch**, **sh**, **ss**, **z**, and sometimes **o**.	fox echo	fox**es** echo**es**
• For most nouns that end in **y**, change the **y** to **i** and then add **–es**. BUT for nouns that end with a vowel and **y**, just add **–s**.	community day	communit**ies** day**s**
• For most nouns that end in **f** or **fe**, change the **f** to **v** and add **–es**. For some nouns that end in **f**, just add **–s**.	leaf cliff	lea**ves** cliff**s**

Read Plural Nouns

Read aloud this passage. Talk to a partner about the plural nouns you find.

> Herbivores are animals that eat plants. In the desert, they may nibble on seeds, flowers, roots, leaves, and grasses.

Write Plural Nouns

Talk to a partner about what you see on pages 162–163. Write a sentence. Include two plural nouns. Compare your sentence with your partner's.

183

Language Focus

Language Frames

• Why do you feel
  _____ ?

• What do you think
  _____ ?

Engage in Conversation

Listen to Jaime and Josie's conversation. Then use **Language Frames** to talk with a partner about the importance of small things in nature.

Why Are Bees Special?

Dialogue

Jaime: You have so many bees! Where do they all live?

Josie: I build beehives for them. We can move closer to see one.

Jaime: I think I'll stay here. Why do you feel it's important to work with bees?

Josie: Bees are important to the food web. They help plants grow.

Jaime: How do bees do that?

Josie: They spread pollen from plant to plant as they look for food inside flowers. Plants need pollen to make seeds.

Jaime: What do you think is the most interesting thing about bees?

Josie: They communicate by dancing. I like to watch them do a waggle dance.

Jaime: When do they do that dance?

Josie: They do a waggle dance to show each other how to get to a good source of food.

Jaime: Who makes sure they have enough food?

Josie: Bees don't need help with that. They can start a hive wherever there are flowering plants nearby.

beehive

🔊 Key Words

The sun helps plants, including those in the ocean, make food. This is called **photosynthesis**. **Chlorophyll** in plants changes the sun's energy into food. Look at this diagram. Use **Key Words** and other words to talk about an ocean food chain.

Key Words

chlorophyll

magnify

microscope

nutrients

photosynthesis

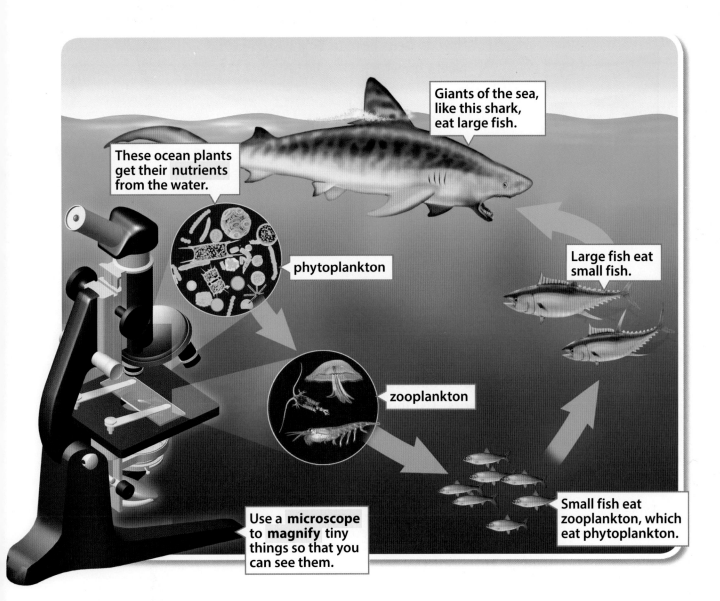

Giants of the sea, like this shark, eat large fish.

These ocean plants get their **nutrients** from the water.

phytoplankton

Large fish eat small fish.

zooplankton

Use a **microscope** to **magnify** tiny things so that you can see them.

Small fish eat zooplankton, which eat phytoplankton.

Talk Together

How do tiny things fit into nature's webs? With a partner, try to use **Language Frames** and **Key Words** to have a conversation about this question.

Main Idea and Details

When someone gives you information, they sometimes give you the big idea, or main idea. Then you ask questions to get the details.

Map and Talk

You can use a tree diagram to keep track of the main idea and details in a conversation. Here's how you build one.

Start with the main point, or main idea, of the section. Write it next to the page where it appears. List the important details.

Tree Diagram

| Page 184 | How do bees help plants grow? | They spread pollen from plant to plant as they look for food. |
| | | Plants need pollen to make seeds. |

Interview a partner about a small plant or animal he or she thinks is important. Use a tree diagram to keep track of the main idea and details.

🔊 More Key Words

Use these words to talk about "Fish of the Future" and "Phyto-Power!"

classify
verb

Amphibians

frog

toad

When you **classify** things, you put them into groups based on their similarities.

investigate
verb

When you **investigate** something, you try to find out more about it.

observe
verb

Observe means to watch someone or something closely. The hikers **observe** birds in the tree.

propose
verb

Propose means to suggest something, such as an idea or plan. He **proposes** the blue one.

specialize
verb

To **specialize** is to learn or know a lot about one thing. He **specializes** in fixing bicycles.

Talk Together

Use a **Key Word** to write a question. Your partner uses a different **Key Word** to answer the question. Use each **Key Word** twice.

Questions	Answers
What animals would you like to investigate?	I propose that we learn more about ocean organisms.

Learn to Determine Importance

To determine what's important, focus on what matters. One way to do this is to find the **main idea**, or what something is mostly about.

Look at the picture of the store window. What is the main idea of the picture? Look for **details** to support your main idea.

When you read, you can identify the **main idea and details**, too.

How to Identify Main Idea and Details

1. Think about the title. Turn the title into a question.

2. Look for information that answers your question. These are the details.

3. Think about how the details answer your question. The answer is your main idea.

My question is _____ .

Detail #1 is _____ .
Detail #2 is _____ .

The main idea is _____ .

Talk Together

Read Jaime's interview. Read the sample. Then use **Language Frames** to tell a partner about other main ideas and details.

Interview

All About Bee-Eaters

Jaime: I know you are a bird expert. What can you tell me about the bee-eater?

Dr. Amos: Bee-eaters are birds. They are easy to see. Males and females are all brightly colored.

Jaime: Where does the bee-eater live?

Dr. Amos: All the different kinds of bee-eaters make their homes in different areas. They are found in Europe, Asia, Africa, and Australia.

Jaime: I think I know why the bird is called the "bee-eater." Does it eat bees?

Dr. Amos: Of course! It also gets **nutrients** from eating wasps and other bugs.

Jaime: How do you know so much about bee-eaters?

Dr. Amos: I **specialize** in bee-eaters. I **investigate** them by **observing** them in the places where they live. First, I **classify** them, and then I write about them.

"My question is, 'What is the bee-eater?'

Detail #1 is the bee-eater is a bird.

Detail #2 is it is brightly colored.

The main idea is the bee-eater is a brightly colored bird."

◄ = A good place to ask a question about a main idea

Read an Interview

Genre

An **interview** gives information and opinions. In an interview, one person asks questions and another person answers them.

Text Features

Charts and **tables** are used to organize information. A chart may take the form of a table, graph, diagram, or picture. A table is a specific kind of chart that shows facts and figures in rows and columns.

title

Sunfish Size Comparisons		
Animal	**Average Length**	**Average Weight**
sea lion	2.7 m (9 ft)	566 kg (1,248 lbs)
sunfish	1.8 m (6 ft)	999 kg (2,202 lbs)
great white shark	4.6 m (15 ft)	2,268 kg (5,000 lbs)
blue whale	29.9 m (98 ft)	99,800 kg (220,021 lbs)

row

column

FISH OF THE
Future

by **Cheryl Block**

▶ **Set a Purpose**
Learn about a unique fish that
is part of the ocean ecosystem.

*When you think of large predators, you may think of **fierce**
lions in the jungle or giant grizzly bears in the forest. In the
ocean, you may think of **streamlined** sharks and powerful
killer whales. But who would think of this funny-looking
sunfish, or Mola mola, as an important predator in the
ocean food web? Dr. Tierney Thys certainly does.*

**Sunfish are predators, but
they will not harm humans if
approached gently.**

fierce dangerous
streamlined smooth, fast

Understanding the Ocean Ecosystem

Dr. Tierney Thys is a marine biologist who has made it her life's work to learn more about the ocean ecosystem. She has focused her research on the sunfish, a unique fish that most people have never even heard about. She uses a variety of technologies, including satellite tracking, to study this giant fish.

▲ **Dr. Tierney Thys has been interested in the ocean since she was a girl.**

Tierney has two goals—to better understand the ocean sunfish and to increase public awareness of ocean conservation. "We need to learn as much as we can about our ocean in order to conserve its great resources for the future. Understanding the **connectedness of** the ocean environment is critical to its health and our survival." In the following interview, Tierney explains her reasons for thinking this way.

connectedness of close relationships between living things in

▶ **Before You Continue**

1. **Use Text Features** Reread the photo captions on pages 192–193. What do you think this interview is about?

2. **Compare** How is a sunfish different from animals that most people picture when they think of fierce predators?

193

What's Special About the Sunfish?

Q: Why did you decide to study the sunfish?

A: I've always been interested in how an animal's shape relates to how it uses its body. Why do animals look the way they do? How does their shape help them? You can see that a tuna's streamlined body is built for speed. I wanted to **investigate** why the sunfish has such an odd body shape.

Basic Body Shapes of Fish

Type	Body Shape	Fish
torpedo (fusiform)	rounded body that **tapers**	
compressed	tall body with flat sides	
depressed	flat body	
eel-like	thin, snake-like body	

◀ This tuna's tapered body is built for speed.

tapers gets smaller toward the back

Parts of a Sunfish

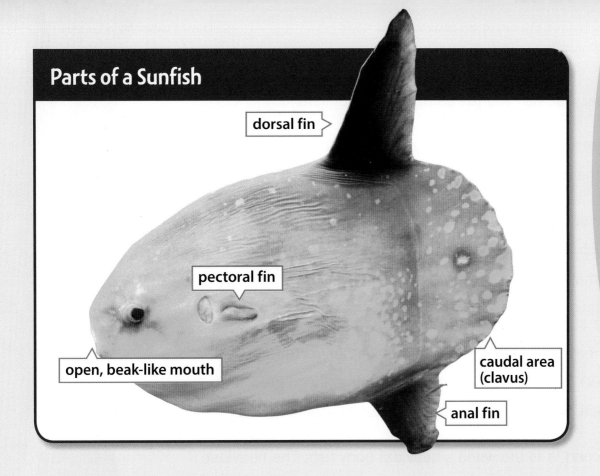

dorsal fin

pectoral fin

open, beak-like mouth

caudal area (clavus)

anal fin

For example, most fish use pectoral and/or caudal fins to propel them through water. In contrast, the sunfish barely uses its small pectoral fins, and does not have a true caudal fin.

Yet this strange shape does not **hinder** the sunfish. By moving its dorsal and anal fins in opposite directions, it swims quite well. It can dive deep in the water many times a day looking for food. Some dives are as deep as 800 meters (2,625 feet).

Another interesting part of the sunfish is its hard, beak-like mouth. Its main food is **jellies**. To eat them, the sunfish simply sucks them in and out of its mouth until they break into easy-to-swallow chunks.

hinder hold back
jellies jellyfish

▶ **Before You Continue**

1. **Main Idea** What is unique about the sunfish's body shape?
2. **Use Text Features** Which of the four basic body shapes of fish does the sunfish have?

Q: What else can you tell us about the sunfish?

A: It gets its common name from its habit of lying on its side at the ocean's surface, as if it is sunning itself.

The sunfish is a floating buffet. It is covered with parasites, which feed on its body. These parasites are food for other animals, such as cleaner fish, and sea birds.

The sunfish holds three world records! As it grows, it increases in weight more than any other **vertebrate**—up to 60 million times its size at **hatching**. If you grew that much, you'd be as big as 30 thousand school buses!

Second, it is the world's heaviest bony fish. The heaviest sunfish ever recorded weighed more than 2,300 kilograms (over 5,000 pounds). That's as heavy as ten grand pianos, or five large cows!

Third, the sunfish produces more eggs at one time than any other vertebrate. Scientists found one mother sunfish carrying **an estimated** 300 million eggs.

Seagulls like this one, like to dine on parasites that cover the sunfish. ▶

vertebrate animal with a backbone
hatching birth
an estimated what they calculated were

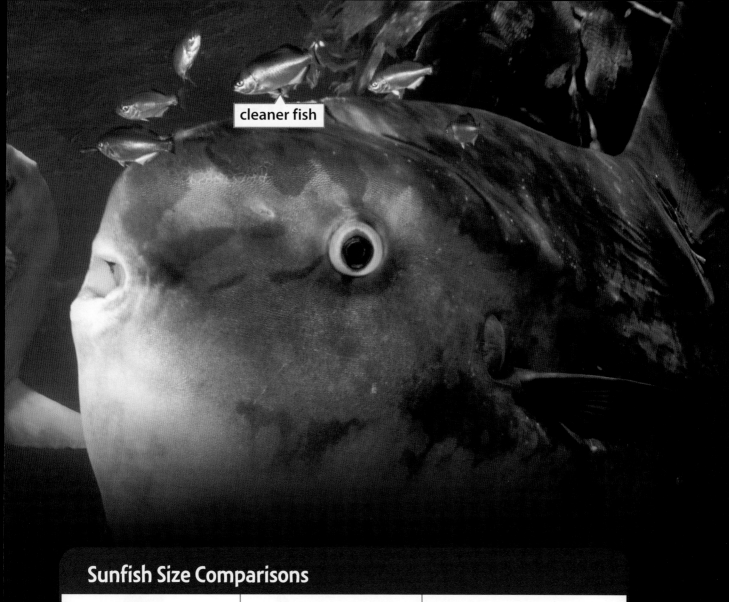

cleaner fish

Sunfish Size Comparisons

Animal	Average Length	Average Weight
sea lion	2.7 m (9 ft)	566 kg (1,248 lbs)
sunfish	1.8 m (6 ft)	999 kg (2,202 lbs)
great white shark	4.6 m (15 ft)	2,268 kg (5,000 lbs)
blue whale	29.9 m (98 ft)	99,800 kg (220,021 lbs)

▲ The sunfish can be compared to some of the largest animals in the ocean.

▶ **Before You Continue**

1. **Details** How does the sunfish help birds and other animals?
2. **Use Text Features** About how many sea lions would equal the weight of one sunfish?

The Sunfish and the Ocean Food Web

Q: How does the sunfish fit into the ocean food web?

A: The sunfish is a carnivorous predator. Its main food is jellies, which eat plankton. It may also eat fish and squid.

The sunfish can also be prey. Smaller, younger sunfish are prey to sea lions, sharks, and killer whales. However, the adult sunfish's huge size helps protect it from most predators, except humans.

Right now, many things are changing the ocean food web. One major factor is our overfishing. We catch and consume too many large predators, like tuna and sharks, as well as their food supply.

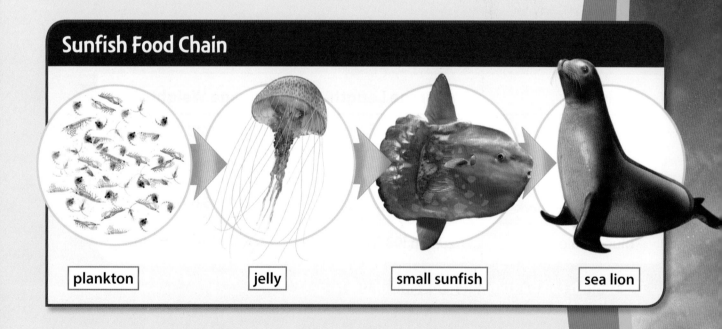

Sunfish Food Chain

| plankton | jelly | small sunfish | sea lion |

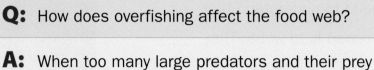

Q: How does overfishing affect the food web?

A: When too many large predators and their prey are caught, jellies can move into their empty **niches**. When jelly populations grow too large, they can compete with other sea creatures for food.

The good news is that the sunfish **specializes** in eating jellies.

These photos show some different jelly **species**.

niches places in the ocean food web
species types

▶ **Before You Continue**

1. **Summarize** How does overfishing affect the ocean food web?
2. **Draw Conclusions** Why could the sunfish become even more important as a carnivore?

Q: Why is it important to us that sunfish eat jellies?

A: To answer this question, we need to understand that jellies are near the bottom of ocean food webs. They eat producers, such as algae, and plant plankton, or phytoplankton.

They also eat zooplankton, or animal plankton. This includes the **larvae** of many different kinds of animals such as fish, crabs, and sponges.

An increase in jellies could mean a decrease in zooplankton. This, in turn, could mean a decrease in many other animals, including the fish that people eat.

By slurping up jellies, the sunfish **has the potential** to keep jelly populations from getting out of control.

larvae babies
has the potential may be able

An Ocean Food Web

killer whale

tuna

sea lion

sunfish

sardines

jelly

zooplankton

phytoplankton

Jellies eat zooplankton, which include the larvae of many animals. Fortunately, sunfish eat jellies.

▶ **Before You Continue**

1. **Main Idea** What could result from an increase in jellies in the ocean?

2. **Use Text Features** Study the diagram. Explain how a sunfish depends on phytoplankton.

Technology Rules!

Q: How do you study the ocean sunfish?

A: We track the sunfish using pop-up satellite tags. These tags are attached to the animal with a dart. The tag contains sensors and a mini-computer that help us track the animal's movement for up to two years. Then the tag releases from the animal's body, floats to the surface, and **uploads data** to a satellite. The data is then downloaded to our computers.

Q: What have you learned from tagging?

A: Tagging lets us see the ocean through the eyes of the fish. We have learned that sunfish make repeated deep dives into **cold** waters but spend most of their time in **warmer** waters. We're also learning about their home ranges and **migration routes**.

pop-up satellite tag

▲ Tierney (right) and fellow scientist, Dr. Dewar, use satellite tags to gather information about the sunfish.

uploads data sends information
cold 1–2° Celsius (34–35° Fahrenheit)
warmer 13–19° Celsius (55–66° Fahrenheit)
migration routes where they go when they leave their home ranges

How to Track a Sunfish

Follow the steps below to learn how Tierney and her team track a sunfish using information from a satellite tag.

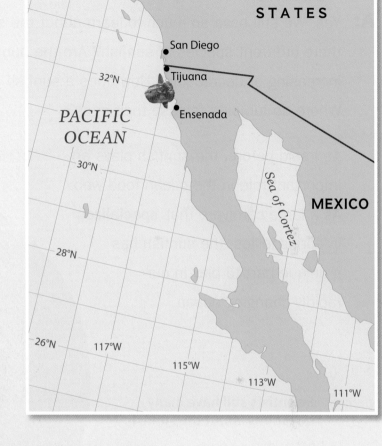

1. Look at the geographical coordinates, or numbers, in the first row of the list below.

Geographical Coordinates

N 32, W 117

N 30, W 117

N 28, W 117

2. Find the horizontal line on the map labeled 32° N.

3. Find the vertical line labeled 117° W.

4. With your fingers, follow both lines until they meet. Notice the sunfish **icon**. This is the first location from which the tag sent data.

5. Look at the next two rows of geographical coordinates. You can use them to find the next two locations from which the tag sent data.

icon symbol

▶ Before You Continue

1. **Summarize** Explain in logical order the process of tracking a sunfish.
2. **Use Text Features** Find where the next two icons belong on the map. In which direction is the sunfish moving?

Fish of the Future

Q: Will you continue to study the sunfish?

A: Yes. We still have so much to learn about the sunfish. Are there different species of sunfish? Are the numbers of sunfish increasing or decreasing? How does a sunfish find food? Where do females release their eggs?

As I said before, the sunfish plays an important role in the ocean food web. As a large carnivore that **specializes** in eating jellies, the sunfish has a unique part to play in our rapidly changing ocean.

Scientists still have many questions about the sunfish. ▶

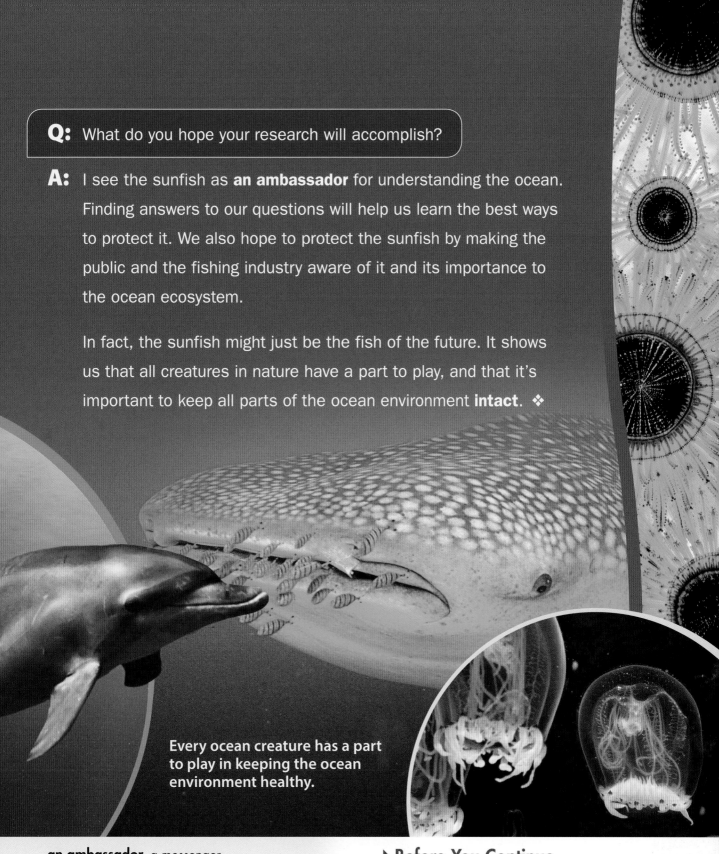

Q: What do you hope your research will accomplish?

A: I see the sunfish as **an ambassador** for understanding the ocean. Finding answers to our questions will help us learn the best ways to protect it. We also hope to protect the sunfish by making the public and the fishing industry aware of it and its importance to the ocean ecosystem.

In fact, the sunfish might just be the fish of the future. It shows us that all creatures in nature have a part to play, and that it's important to keep all parts of the ocean environment **intact**. ❖

Every ocean creature has a part to play in keeping the ocean environment healthy.

an ambassador a messenger
intact together

▶ **Before You Continue**

1. **Paraphrase** In your own words, explain how Tierney helps protect the sunfish.
2. **Synthesize** Do you think there will be more sunfish in the future? Why or why not?

Think and Respond

Key Words

chlorophyll	nutrients
classify	observe
investigate	photosynthesis
magnify	propose
microscope	specialize

Talk About It

1. What is Tierney Thys like, based on her **interview**?

2. With a partner, have a **conversation** about the work that Tierney Thys does and what it might be like to have her job, based on what you read. Think of questions you might ask her to start your conversation.

   Tierney probably spends a lot of time _____.

   I would/would not enjoy _____.

3. Compare the role of the ocean sunfish to the role of jellies in the ocean food web.

Write About It

Write a paragraph that describes the kind of scientist you would most like to be. What would you like to **investigate**?

If I were a scientist, I would **specialize** in _____. I would investigate _____.

I think _____.

Main Idea and Details

Use a tree diagram to keep track of the main idea and details of each section of the interview. Each section begins with a heading.

Tree Diagram

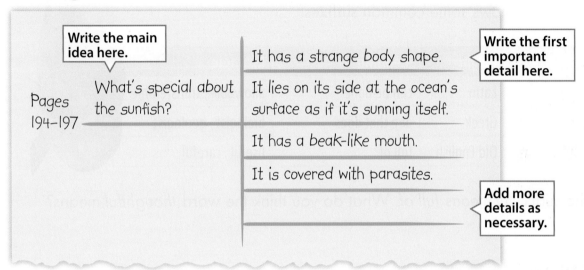

Write the main idea here.

Pages 194–197

What's special about the sunfish?

It has a strange body shape.

Write the first important detail here.

It lies on its side at the ocean's surface as if it's sunning itself.

It has a beak-like mouth.

It is covered with parasites.

Add more details as necessary.

Now use your tree diagram to summarize the interview to a partner.

The interview is mainly about _____ .

Fluency

Practice reading with expression. Rate your reading.

Why should we care about the small things in nature? Write a poem that praises something small in nature. Include **Key Words** in your poem. Share your poem with the class.

Suffixes

Many English words end with a **suffix**, or a short word part. Many of these English suffixes came from Latin, Greek, or Old English. Sometimes knowing the meaning of the suffix can help you predict the meaning of the word.

This chart shows some common suffixes.

Suffix	Origin	Meaning	Example
-able	Latin	can be done	allow**able** , transfer**able**
-ist	Greek	one that does	biolog**ist** , geolog**ist**
-ful	Old English	full of	use**ful** , care**ful**

The suffix *-ful* means *full of*. What do you think the word *thoughtful* means?

Try It Together

Read the sentences. Then answer the questions. Use the chart above to help you.

> Marine botanists study plant life in the ocean—from spiky sea urchins, to bountiful seaweed. They think studying plants is enjoyable and useful work.

1. **Look for the Latin suffix in the word *enjoyable*. What do you think enjoyable means?**

   A not enjoyable

   B one who enjoys things

   C a fun object

   D can be enjoyed

2. **Look for the Greek suffix *-ist*. What do you think botanist means?**

   A an ocean plant

   B one that studies botany

   C the study of plant life

   D a male scientist

Phyto-Power!

by Mary M. Cerullo

Imagine that you are going on an undersea **voyage** to meet the most important creatures on Earth. You step into your submarine. Then you shrink, becoming smaller than the period at the end of this sentence. You look through your porthole and see strange, amazing life forms: phytoplankton. These tiny creatures are responsible for all other life in the sea. They also help make the oxygen we breathe.

In this submarine, people can easily observe the underwater world. ▶

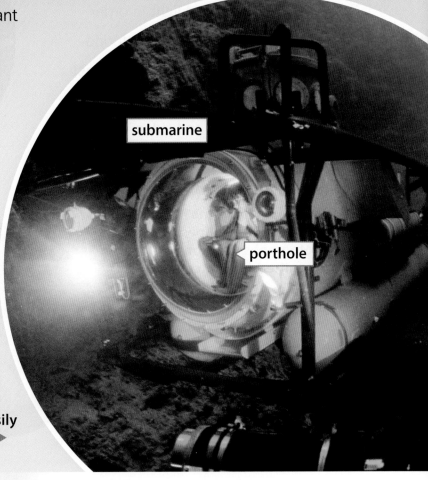

submarine

porthole

voyage journey; trip

▶ **Before You Continue**

1. **Main Idea** Why are phytoplankton important?
2. **Synthesize** What can you compare the size of phytoplankton to? What are they smaller than, according to the text?

Tiny Drifters

Phytoplankton are tiny, microscopic, plant-like organisms. They don't look like the plants on land. They have no roots, stems, or leaves. Instead, phytoplankton resemble spiky balls, links on a bracelet, spaceships, and other oddly-shaped objects.

Phytoplankton are incredibly small. One spoonful of sea water can hold a million phytoplankton.

Phytoplankton need light in order to grow, so they are usually found near the surface of the water. Most of them drift through the ocean on **currents**, waves, and **tides**.

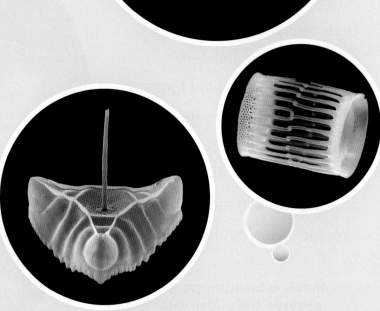

Phytoplankton come in many different shapes. These photographs show phytoplankton magnified by a microscope. ▶

currents rivers of moving water
tides water that gets higher, then lower

Food and Oxygen Factories

At the surface of the ocean, where phytoplankton live, there is sunlight, water, and carbon dioxide. These three things allow phytoplankton to make their own food.

Like plants, phytoplankton have a chemical called **chlorophyll**. Chlorophyll **captures** sunlight and changes it into **sugars and starches**. This chemical reaction is called **photosynthesis**. Photosynthesis also **produces** oxygen and releases it into the water and air.

Phytoplankton Photosynthesis

energy from the sun

carbon dioxide from the air

oxygen into the air

carbon dioxide from the water

oxygen into the water

phytoplankton

captures takes in
sugars and starches food
produces makes

▶ **Before You Continue**

1. **Make Comparisons** How are phytoplankton and land plants the same? How are they different?

2. **Use Text Features** Where do phytoplankton get the carbon dioxide they need for **photosynthesis**?

Feeding the Ocean Food Chain

Directly or indirectly, phytoplankton feed everything else in the ocean, even whales. Here's how this happens. Tiny animals called zooplankton eat phytoplankton. Zooplankton, in turn, may be eaten by small fishes. These small fishes are eaten by bigger fishes. Big fishes are eaten by sharks, some kinds of whales, and other large ocean predators.

In order to feel full, an adult killer whale may need to eat over 135 kilograms (300 pounds) of fish a day. These fish have eaten zooplankton. Each zooplankter (single zooplankton) has fed on as many as 130 thousand phytoplankton. Therefore, one meal for a killer whale may represent more than 400 billion phytoplankton!

An Ocean Food Chain

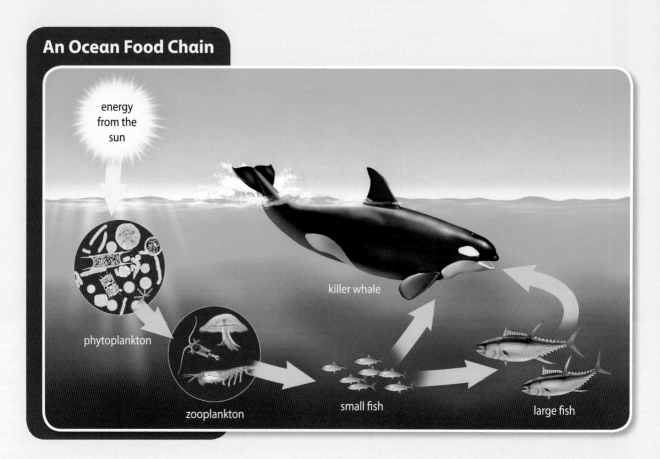

energy from the sun

phytoplankton

zooplankton

killer whale

small fish

large fish

Have You Thanked Phytoplankton Today?

Perhaps most important of all, phytoplankton help us breathe. About half of the world's oxygen may come from phytoplankton. That means every other breath you take is probably because of the work of phytoplankton.

So the next time you are amazed by a giant killer whale, are impressed by the beautiful green ocean, or take a breath of fresh, oxygen-rich air, don't forget to thank phytoplankton. They helped make all these things possible! ❖

All forms of ocean life depend on phytoplankton, including this killer whale. ▶

▶ **Before You Continue**

1. **Main Idea** How do phytoplankton help people?
2. **Details** What organisms connect phytoplankton to whales?

Key Words	
chlorophyll	nutrients
classify	observe
investigate	photosynthesis
magnify	propose
microscope	specialize

Compare Genres

"Phyto-Power!" is a **science article**. "Fish of the Future" is an **interview**. How are the two selections alike? How are they different? Make a chart to compare the two selections. Think about each selection's purpose, text structure, and text features.

Comparison Chart

	Science Article	Interview
Purpose Is the purpose to inform, entertain, persuade, or tell readers how to do something?		
Text Structure	Main Idea and Details	Questions and Answers
Text Feature	Photos *Yes* Tables Charts Illustrations Headings Maps Diagrams	Photos *Yes* Tables Charts Illustrations Headings Maps Diagrams

How are humans connected to ocean life? Think about the science article and the interview with Tierney Thys. Use **Key Words** to talk about your ideas.

More Plural Nouns

There are different ways to form **plural nouns**.

Grammar Rules — More Plural Nouns

• Some nouns use the same form for "one" and "more than one."	sheep → sheep
• Some nouns have special spellings for "more than one."	tooth → teeth child → children woman → women
• **Collective nouns** name groups of people, animals, or things.	groups of people: **class**, **family**, **team** groups of animals: **school**, **litter**, **pack** groups of things: **mail**, **money**, **trash**

Read Plural Nouns

Read this passage based on "Phyto-Power!" Find three nouns that have the same form for "one" and "more than one."

> Think of the thin layer of water at the surface of the ocean. Here there is sunlight, water, and carbon dioxide.

Write Plural Nouns

Write two sentences about the photographs on page 210. Compare your sentences to a partner's.

215

Write As a Reporter

Write an Interview

Interview someone who has expert knowledge of animals and nature.
Write an article to share what you learn.

Study a Model

In an interview, you gather information by asking another person questions.
Read the results of Rachel's interview with an animal control officer.

The title and **first paragraph** introduce the person who was interviewed.

Pam Marks, Animal Control
by Rachel Grant

Pam Marks is an animal control officer for the city. I asked her about the coyote problem we've been having.

Q. **Why have coyotes come to the city?**
A. **In a way, we've invited them!** As cities grow, the coyotes' habitats get smaller. So they come to the city, where they have easy access to food, water, and shelter.

Rachel's **questions** flow naturally.

Q. **How dangerous are coyotes?**
A. **They can be very dangerous.** They'll steal small pets, but they will also attack larger animals and even people. Sometimes they bring disease.

The answers are the person's exact words.

Q. **What can we do to keep them away?**
A. Keep garbage cans sealed. Make sure small animals are inside at night, when coyotes like to hunt. In other words, **don't make the coyotes want to visit you!**

Prewrite

1. **Choose a Topic** What questions do you have about animals and how they live? Work with a partner to choose a good topic and person to interview.

Language Frames	
Tell Your Ideas	**Respond to Ideas**
• I want to Know about _____ .	• Who would Know about _____ ?
• I've always wondered how animals live in _____ .	• I'm curious about _____ , too. Can you also ask about _____ ?
• _____ seem like interesting animals. I'd like to find out more about them.	• _____ doesn't sound like a good interview topic. Do you have other ideas?

2. **Gather Information** Use a chart to help you prepare your interview questions ahead of time. Then take notes or record the interview.

Who?	Pam Marks
What?	What can we do to Keep coyotes away?
Where?	
When?	
Why?	Why do they come to the city?
How?	How dangerous are coyotes?

3. **Get Organized** Review your notes or recording. Choose the most important or interesting questions and answers.

Draft

Use the questions and answers you chose to write your article. Introduce the person you interviewed first, and then write the questions and answers in a logical order.

Revise

1. **Read, Retell, Respond** Read your draft aloud to a partner. Use the words *question* and *answer* so your partner will understand which parts you are reading. Then you can both talk about your interview and how to improve it.

Language Frames

Retell	**Make Suggestions**
• You interviewed _____ . • Some of the things you asked about were _____ . • The most interesting information I heard was _____ .	• I didn't understand _____ . Is that exactly what the person said? • The questions might flow better if you moved _____ to _____ .

---

2. **Make Changes** Think about your draft and your partner's suggestions. Use revision marks to make your changes.

   • Are your questions in a logical order? Would a different order make more sense?

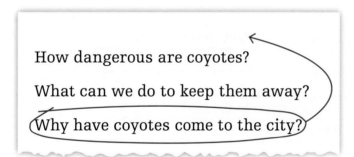

Edit and Proofread

Work with a partner to edit and proofread your interview. Pay special attention to plural nouns. Be sure to start sentences with capital letters and end them with periods.

Present

On Your Own Make a final copy of your interview. Read it aloud to your classmates. You could also invite the person you interviewed to visit and answer additional questions.

Presentation Tips	
If you are the speaker...	**If you are the listener...**
Pause between questions and answers. Speak clearly.	What did you learn that you didn't know? Take notes on new information.
Show pictures of the animal you asked about.	Keep track of anything you didn't understand. Then ask questions.

In a Group Use the results of your interviews to create a special-edition newspaper. Add pictures and other articles related to your topics. Print copies of your newspaper to share around school.

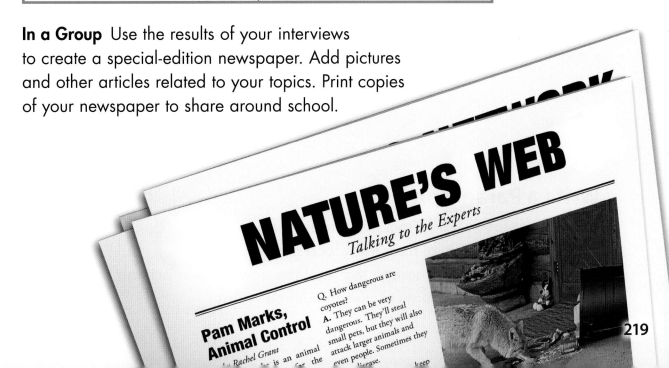

NATURE'S WEB
Talking to the Experts

Pam Marks,
Animal Control

Q. How dangerous are coyotes?
A. They can be very dangerous. They'll steal small pets, but they will also attack larger animals and even people. Sometimes they

Talk Together

In this unit, you found lots of answers to the **Big Question**. Now, use your concept map to discuss the **Big Question** with the class.

Concept Map

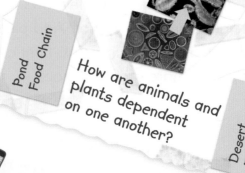

Pond Food Chain

How are animals and plants dependent on one another?

Desert Food Chain

Write a Paragraph

Choose two food chains from the concept map. Then choose one animal from each food chain. Write a comparison-contrast paragraph that explains how the two animals are alike and different in their roles in nature's webs.

Share Your Ideas

Choose one of these ways to share your ideas about the **Big Question**.

Write It!

Make a Food Chain

Research other plants and animals that live in the desert or the ocean. Make a new food chain. Find or draw pictures of the plants and animals in your food chain. Write captions to go with the pictures.

The Top of the Ocean Food Chain

Talk About It!

Perform a Play

With a small group, talk about how you could turn "Coyote and Badger" into a play. Work together to rewrite part of the story as a play. Then perform it for the class.

Do It!

Act Out a Food Web

Make a food web card for each student. Give a ball of string to the person who has the "Sun" card. Pass the string from the sun to each producer. Then pass the string between the producers and the herbivores. Finally, pass the string between the herbivores and the carnivores. Watch the food web grow.

Write It!

Write an Ode

An ode is a short poem written to praise its subject. Choose your favorite animal from this unit, and write an ode in praise of this animal. Say what is great about the animal and why it is important to the world. Read your ode aloud to the class.

Unit 4

Justice

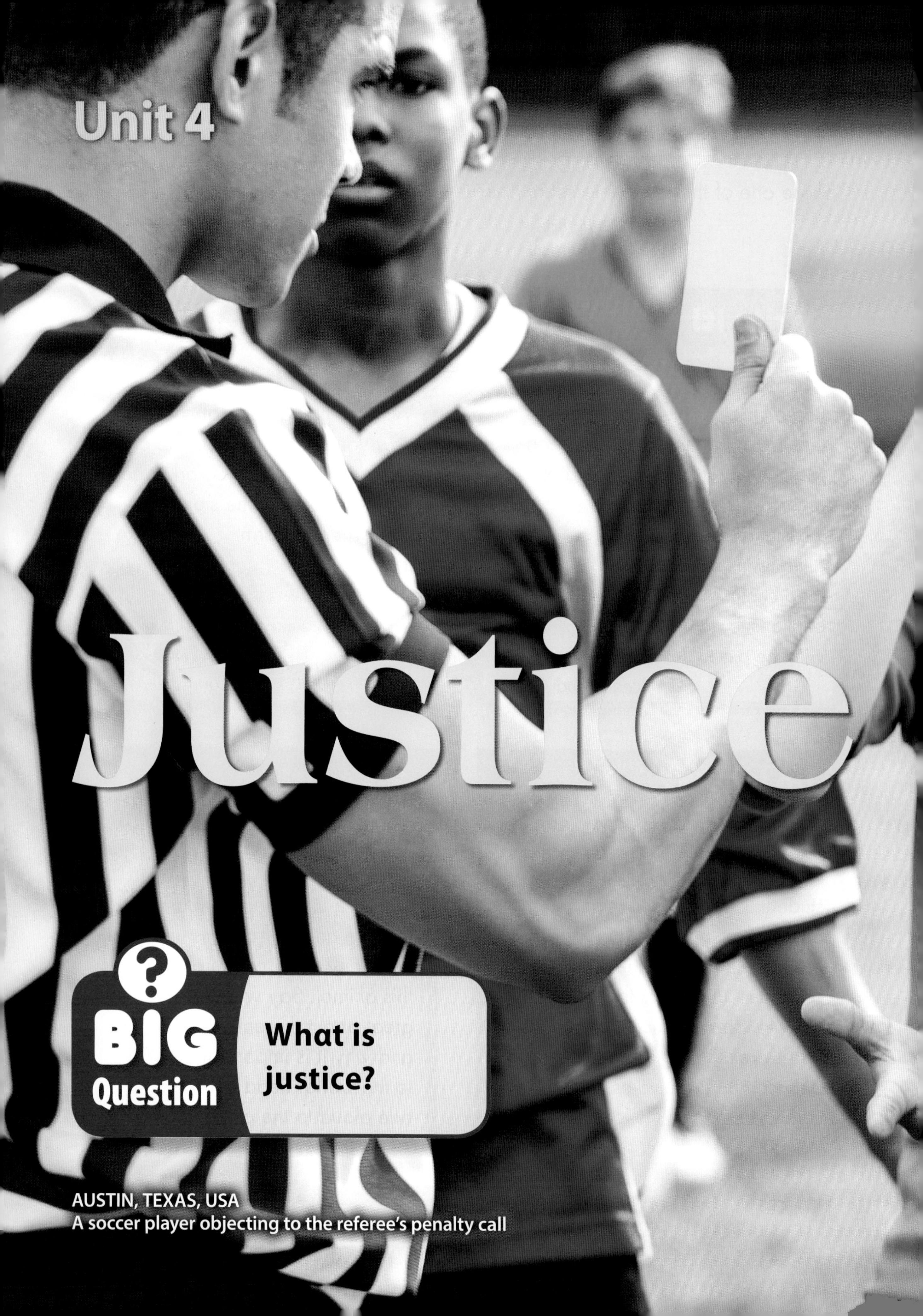

BIG Question

What is justice?

AUSTIN, TEXAS, USA
A soccer player objecting to the referee's penalty call

Share What You Know

1 **Think** about an experience that was fair. Write it on a note card. Label it "Fair."

2 **Think** about an experience that was unfair. Write it on a note card. Label it "Unfair."

3 **Exchange** your cards with a partner. **Share** the experiences with the class.

Do It!

UNFAIR
Someone cut in line at the movie theater.

Justify

Matt and Salvador are talking about someone they think
is a hero. Listen to their dialogue. Then use **Language
Frames** to tell a partner if you agree with their choice and why.

An American Hero

Dialogue

Matt: I just read a story based on the life of Frederick Douglass.
He was born into slavery and escaped to freedom.

Salvador: I know about him! He escaped by boarding a train
dressed as a sailor. He made it all the way to
the North.

Matt: Then, he became an abolitionist. I think he is an
American hero. I believe this because he wanted all
people to be free.

Salvador: Right! If not, then people's lives are never their own.

Matt: And so, I'm going to do my book report on
Frederick Douglass.

Key Words

🔊 **Key Words**

Look at the pictures. Use **Key Words** to talk about slavery
in the United States.

Key Words
abolish
emancipation
escape
law
plantation
slavery

During **slavery**, many Africans were
forced to work on **plantations**. The
work was hard. They were not paid.

Before **emancipation**, some
enslaved people **escaped**
from, or left, the plantation.

Many enslaved people used secret
paths to travel north, where slavery
was against the **law**. Along the way,
people helped them.

Later, the Thirteenth Amendment
to the Constitution **abolished**, or
ended, slavery.

Talk Together

Some enslaved people risked their lives for freedom. What would you risk
for freedom? With a group, use **Language Frames** from page 224 and the
Key Words to justify your answer.

225

Theme

The main message of a story is its **theme**. To identify theme, think about all the parts of a story. Then think about the message the author wants you to learn or discover.

Look at the pictures from the story that Matt read. The title is *Frederick Douglass' Civil War*.

Douglass speaks out against slavery.

Douglass writes about the war.

The 54th Regiment goes to war.

Map and Talk

You can use a theme chart to help you discover the theme of a story. First, write down clues you find from the title. Then write clues from the characters, the setting, and the plot. Finally, use the clues to find the **theme**.

Theme Chart

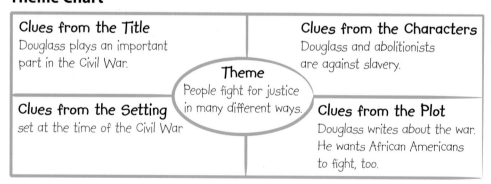

Talk with your partner about a television show you have seen about a hero. Your partner can make a theme chart. Use the chart to find the theme of the TV Show.

🔊 More Key Words

Use these words to talk about "Crossing Bok Chitto: A Choctaw Tale of Friendship and Freedom" and "Journey To Freedom."

distinguish
verb

Distinguish means to tell the difference between two things. It's hard to **distinguish** Chris from his twin, Joe.

equality
noun

When people have **equality,** they all have the same rights. **Equality** makes things even.

freedom
noun

Freedom is being able to say, think, and do what you want. A bird has the **freedom** to fly.

risk
verb

When you **risk** something, you are in danger of losing or harming it.

route
noun

A **route** is a path to get from one place to another. Use a map to find a **route** to the ocean.

Talk Together

Work with a partner. Role-play a scene in which two people risk something for justice. Use at least two **Key Words** in the scene.

> Enslaved people **risked** their lives in order to reach **freedom.**

227

Learn to Make Inferences

Look at the cartoon of Matt and Salvador. Think about the details you see in the picture and what you already know about the library. Figure out, or **make an inference** about, what will happen next.

When you read, you can **make inferences**, too.

How to Make Inferences

	1. Look for details in the text.	I read _____ .
	2. Think about what you already know about the details and the topic.	I know _____ .
	3. Put your ideas together. What else can you figure out about the text?	And so _____ .

Talk Together

Read Matt's personal narrative about standing up for justice. Read the sample inference. Then use **Language Frames** to tell a partner about your inferences.

Personal Narrative

My Grandfather, My Hero

The other day, I read about a man who stood up for what was right. That made me think of my grandfather. He stood up for justice fifty years ago and even helped change the **law**. Back then, some schools were separate and not equal. My grandfather marched with many other Americans. He spoke out for **equality** between African-American and Caucasian students.

My grandfather said that **emancipation** from **slavery** happened more than one hundred years ago. But, even in the 1950s and 1960s, African Americans were still not free. They still had to speak up for their **freedom**. He showed me pictures of things that happened when African Americans would **risk** trying to ride at the front of a bus, or eat at a "Whites only" lunch counter. Grandpa got very quiet, and tears were in his eyes. ◄

He showed me a picture of Al, an African-American student from the North who helped his mother vote for the first time. He was one of many people who came from the North. They traveled many **routes** through the South to help African Americans vote. ◄ They risked their lives and were very brave. Al taught Grandpa to **distinguish** between right and wrong, and to stand up for what is right. I can see how important that lesson is even today!

"I read that schools were not equal.

I know that 'equality' means being treated equally.

And so African Americans and Caucasians were not treated equally."

◄ = a good place to stop and make an inference

229

Read a Story

Genre

A **tale** is a story that is told over and over again before it is written down. This tale is based on historical events.

Characters and Setting

Characters are the people in a story. The setting of a story is *when* and *where* it takes place. This story takes place before the Civil War, near a plantation in Mississippi.

Little Mo

Martha Tom

Crossing Bok Chitto

A Choctaw Tale of Friendship and Freedom

by **Tim Tingle**

▶ **Set a Purpose**
Martha Tom and Little Mo are
from different cultures. How do
they meet?

There is a river called Bok Chitto that flows through Mississippi. In the days before the **War Between the States**, in the days before the **Trail of Tears**, Bok Chitto was a boundary. On one side of the river lived the Choctaws, a nation of **Indian** people. On the other side lived the **plantation** owners and the people they had enslaved. If an enslaved person **escaped** and made his way across Bok Chitto, that person was free. That was the **law**.

One Sunday morning during this time, a Choctaw momma woke her daughter.

"Martha Tom, get up! I have a wedding to cook for today. Take this basket and fill it with blackberries."

But Martha Tom couldn't find any blackberries on the Choctaw side of the river, so she did something she'd been told never to do—she went **crossing** Bok Chitto. The only way to cross Bok Chitto in those days was a stone path just beneath the surface of the river. Only the Choctaws knew it was there, for the Choctaws had built it.

War Between the States Civil War
Trail of Tears Native Americans in the South
  were forced to leave their homes
Indian Native American
crossing across

Martha Tom found a patch of blackberries on the **plantation** side of the river. She filled her basket and started for home, but she soon realized that she was lost. She tried to find the river, but instead she walked deeper into the woods.

stone path

She came upon a clearing filled with logs that looked like benches. A skinny, dark-skinned man with a cane stepped out of the trees. He climbed onto a stump and called out, "We are **bound for the Promised Land**! Oh, who will go with me?"

What happened next would change Martha Tom's life forever.

A group of enslaved people stepped from behind the trees where they were hiding. "We will go with you," they replied.

"We are bound for the Promised Land!"

It was the calling together of the forbidden church, deep in those Mississippi woods. The people began to sing. Martha Tom had never heard music like this before, but it **touched her deeply**.

bound for the Promised Land going to a place where we will be free

touched her deeply filled her with strong feelings

Then something else touched her—on the shoulder. She looked up to see the biggest man she had ever seen.

"You're lost, little girl?" he said in a **deep** voice. "You're Choctaw, from across Bok Chitto?"

Martha Tom nodded.

"What is your name?"

"Martha Tom."

"Well, Martha Tom, I'll get my son to take you back to the river. Little Mo!" he called.

A boy appeared. "Little Mo, this girl is lost. She is Choctaw from across Bok Chitto. Take her to the **riverbank** and she can get home from there."

"Daddy, I **better not**," Little Mo said. "The men from the **plantation** house told us to stay away from the river."

---

deep low
riverbank side of the river
better not don't think I should do that

▶ **Before You Continue**

1. **Summarize** How do Martha Tom and Little Mo meet?

2. **Make Inferences** Why do you think the **plantation** owners want the people they had enslaved to stay away from the river?

▶ Predict
Do you think Little Mo will take
Martha Tom to the river? Explain.

His father **knelt down** and said, "Son, there is a way to move amongst them where they won't even notice you. It's like **you're invisible**. You move not too fast, not too slow, eyes to the ground, away you go! Now give it a try and get this little girl home!"

So Little Mo took Martha Tom by the hand and off they went, not too fast, not too slow, eyes to the ground, away you go!

They walked right in front of the **plantation** house porch, where the owners were sitting. But no one **paid them any mind**.

knelt down got on his knees
you're invisible no one can see you
paid them any mind noticed them

When they arrived at the river, Martha Tom took Little Mo by the hand and the two of them went crossing Bok Chitto to the Choctaw side.

Even before they stepped from the stones to the earth, Little Mo heard the sound of chanting. He thought it must be the heartbeat of the earth itself. It was the old men calling the Choctaws to the wedding ceremony.

"Way, hey ya hey ya
You a hey you ay
A hey ya a hey ya!

Way, hey ya hey ya
You a hey you ay
A hey ya a hey ya!"

Little Mo had never heard music like this before, but it touched him deeply.

Then something else touched them both—on the shoulder. It was Martha Tom's mother!

"Little girl, you have been crossing Bok Chitto! You take him to the river and come right back!"

Martha Tom knew her mother could **cackle** like a crow on the outside, while inside she would **coo** like a dove with love for her daughter. She took Little Mo to the river and showed him how to cross **on his own**. And so began a friendship that would last for years.

Every Sunday morning, Martha Tom would cross Bok Chitto. She sat with Little Mo's family in church. She sang the songs in English, and then she sang them in Choctaw on her way home.

cackle shout; yell
coo sing
on his own by himself

Then one day, **trouble came**. Twenty enslaved people were going to be sold. The men were called together to listen to the names being read. Little Mo's mother was on that list.

Little Mo's father wondered how to tell his family.

After supper, he motioned for them to be still. Feeling his knees grow weak, he said, "Your mother has been sold."

"Nooo!" she cried. The children began to cry, too.

"This is our last evening together!" he said. "Stop your crying. I want every one of you to find something small and **precious** to give your mother to remember you by."

No one moved.

trouble came there was a big problem
precious special

▶ **Before You Continue**

1. **Paraphrase** How did Little Mo get Martha Tom home? In your own words, explain the advice his father gave him and how it helped.

2. **Theme** What is the effect of **slavery** on Little Mo's family at this point in the story?

▶ **Predict**
What might Little Mo's family do
to solve their problem?

Then Little Mo said, "Daddy, there is a way we can stay together. We can go crossing Bok Chitto."

"Son, they'll have the dogs guarding the river."

"Daddy, we can go like you taught me—not too fast, not too slow, eyes to the ground, away you go! Daddy, we have to try."

Hope filled his father's heart. "You are right, son. We have to try."

They packed quickly, but they were not quick enough.

The men in the **plantation** house saw them working late. They called for the guards with the dogs, the **lanterns,** and the guns, and they surrounded that little house.

Little Mo's daddy said to his family, "This night's journey is about **faith**. It is about **freedom**. We will go out the front door."

lanterns lights
faith believing we will be OK

And so they did—not too fast, not too slow, eyes to the ground, away you go!

Then something remarkable happened. They walked into the **circle of lanterns**, but even the dogs did not know they were there. It was like they were invisible.

Soon they stood on the banks of Bok Chitto. Little Mo said, "Daddy, I've never been here at night. I can't get us across!"

His father said, "Son, we call you Little Mo. But you know that your real name is Moses. Now, Moses, get us across that water!"

circle of lanterns light

Little Mo dipped his arms into the chilly waters till he found the stone path. Quick as a bird, he **flew** across the stones and **burst** into Martha Tom's home.

"We are trying to cross the river," he said. "The **plantation** men are **after us**. Can you help us?"

Martha Tom's mother jumped out of bed.

"Son, hide your family in the bushes near the river. You'll know when to come across. Go! I have work to do!"

She went to every home in that village and called inside, "Women! Put on your white dresses! Bring a candle and meet me at the river."

And this is what happened.

flew ran
burst entered without knocking
after us trying to catch us

The guards stood on the **plantation** side of the river with
their dogs, lanterns, and guns. Suddenly, they saw **emerging
from** the white fog on the Choctaw side a group of women
dressed in white. The Choctaw women carried candles that **cast
a glow around** their faces.

Rising from the bushes, the guards saw seven
people **escaping**. They lifted their guns to **fire**.

They never shot their guns that night, for stepping out of
the group of women they saw the most beautiful little girl. Her
right hand held a candle, her left hand was outstretched, and it
looked like she was walking on the water!

emerging from coming out of
cast a glow around shined light on
fire shoot

Martha Tom was singing a song she had learned at the church, but now she sang it in Choctaw.

"Nitak ishtayo pikmano
Chissus ut minitit.
Umala holitopama
Chihot aya lashke!
We are bound for the Promised Land!"

Then Martha Tom led Little Mo and his family across Bok Chitto. The family was never seen on the **plantation** side again.

The **descendants** of those people still talk about that night. The Choctaws talk about the bravery of that little girl, Martha Tom. The dark-skinned people talk about the faith of that little boy, Moses. But maybe the white people tell it best. They talk about the night their **forefathers** witnessed seven enslaved people, walking on the water—to **freedom**! ❖

descendants grandchildren and great-grandchildren

forefathers grandparents and great-grandparents

▶**Before You Continue**

1. **Confirm Prediction** What do the guards think the family is doing? How is the family really crossing Bok Chitto?

2. **Theme** What lesson can you learn from Martha Tom and Little Mo's experience?

Meet the Author

Tim Tingle

AWARD WINNER

Tim Tingle is a member of the Choctaw Nation of Oklahoma. He wrote "Crossing Bok Chitto" to honor all the Native Americans who helped enslaved people escape.

Tim got the idea for the story when he visited a Choctaw elder in Mississippi. The wise old man told Tim about a family who helped people escape from slavery.

Tim turned the elder's words into a story that he hopes others will pass along. In this way, an important piece of Choctaw history will not be forgotten.

"As long as our stories are told, we can be Choctaw forever."

–Tim Tingle

Writing Tip

The narrator uses old-fashioned language like "went crossing," "no one paid them any mind," and "trouble came," to help set the time, place, and mood, or feeling, of the story. Write the first part of a story you know. Use language that helps the reader envision the setting and feel the mood.

Key Words

abolish	law
distinguish	plantation
emancipation	risk
equality	route
escape	slavery
freedom	

Talk About It

1. What details in this **tale** do you think are real? Which are not? How do you know?

2. What did Little Mo and his family **risk** when they decided to cross Bok Chitto? Do you think it was a good idea? **Justify** your answer.

3. What did the Choctaw people believe about **slavery** and **emancipation**? Use details from the story to explain how you know.

   I read _____ . I know _____ . And so _____ .

Write About It

What might Little Mo say to Martha Tom after his family **escapes** to **freedom**? Write a letter from Little Mo to Martha Tom. Use **Key Words** to thank her for her help.

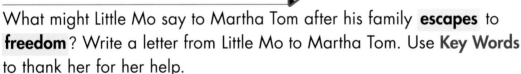

_____ , 1820

Dear Martha Tom,

Now my family and I are _____ .
Thank you for _____ .
We will never forget _____ .

Your friend,
Little Mo

Theme

Use the theme chart to find the theme of "Crossing Bok Chitto."

Theme Chart

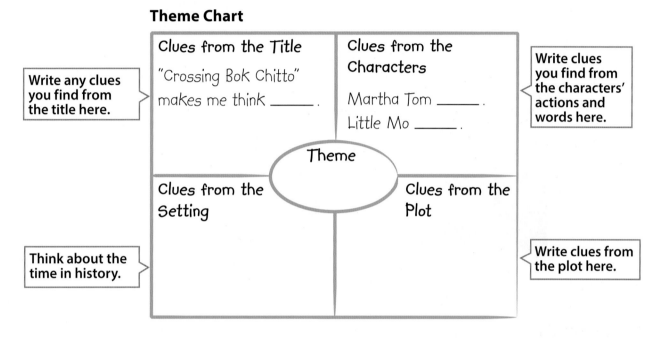

Write any clues you find from the title here.

Clues from the Title

"Crossing Bok Chitto" makes me think _____ .

Clues from the Characters

Martha Tom _____ .
Little Mo _____ .

Write clues you find from the characters' actions and words here.

Theme

Clues from the Setting

Think about the time in history.

Clues from the Plot

Write clues from the plot here.

Now use your theme chart as you retell the story to a partner. Tell them what the theme is and explain how you identified it. Use **Key Words** in your retelling.

The theme for this story is _____ .

Fluency

Practice reading with expression. Rate your reading.

Talk Together

What did Martha Tom **risk** for justice? Write about a person you know who experienced injustice. What did they do about it? Use **Key Words** in your paragraph. Share the paragraph with the class.

Antonyms

Antonyms are words with opposite meanings. The word pair *slavery* and *freedom* are antonyms. Sometimes antonyms are used in analogies. Analogies are word pairs that share a common relationship. Look at this analogy.

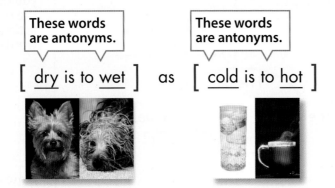

These words are antonyms.

These words are antonyms.

[<u>dry</u> is to <u>wet</u>] as [<u>cold</u> is to <u>hot</u>]

A word analogy shows how two words relate to each other. When you see word analogies on a test, it is your job to figure out the relationship between the sets of word pairs. How would you complete this analogy?

[<u>abolish</u> is to <u>start</u>] as [<u>sadness</u> is to _____]

Try It Together

Read each item. Choose the word that best completes the analogy.

1. **<u>enslaved</u> is to <u>free</u> as <u>safe</u> is to _____**

   A challenging

   B dangerous

   C comfortable

   D unfriendly

2. **<u>sharp</u> is to <u>dull</u> as <u>decrease</u> is to _____**

   A plain

   B evident

   C increase

   D slavery

Making Connections Learn about real people who took risks for **freedom**.

Genre A **history article** is nonfiction. It can be about people, places, and events in the past.

Journey to Freedom

by **Peter Winkler**

Before the Civil War, **slavery** was **legal** in southern states. It was not legal in the northern states, Canada, or Mexico. So enslaved people who were running away often traveled hundreds of miles to reach **freedom**. Many used a **network** called the Underground Railroad.

▲ This group of people escaping slavery worked together to find freedom.

legal allowed by **law**
network group of people

▶ **Before You Continue**

1. **Make Inferences** Why do you think people **escaping slavery** had to use a special network to get away?
2. **Summarize** Why did most enslaved people travel north to find freedom?

Underground Railroad

The Underground Railroad did not have trains or **railway tracks**. It was a group of free people who helped those who were enslaved. As they traveled the hundreds of miles to reach **freedom**, people escaping **slavery** would stop at safe homes or other buildings called "stations." There, people welcomed them with a meal and a place to rest. As the runaways moved from one station to the next, they were accompanied by a "**conductor**" who made sure they arrived safely at the next **destination**. At the end of their journey, the formerly enslaved people started new lives as free people.

Runaways faced great dangers when they **escaped**. They could be **captured** and sent back to slavery. The people who helped them faced great dangers, too. They **risked** prison and even death to help people escape.

▲ Horace Alfred Ford was a conductor on the Underground Railroad. He helped hide runaways in "stations" like this house in Canesto, New York.

railway tracks roads for trains
conductor guide
destination stopping place
captured caught

Routes Along the Underground Railroad

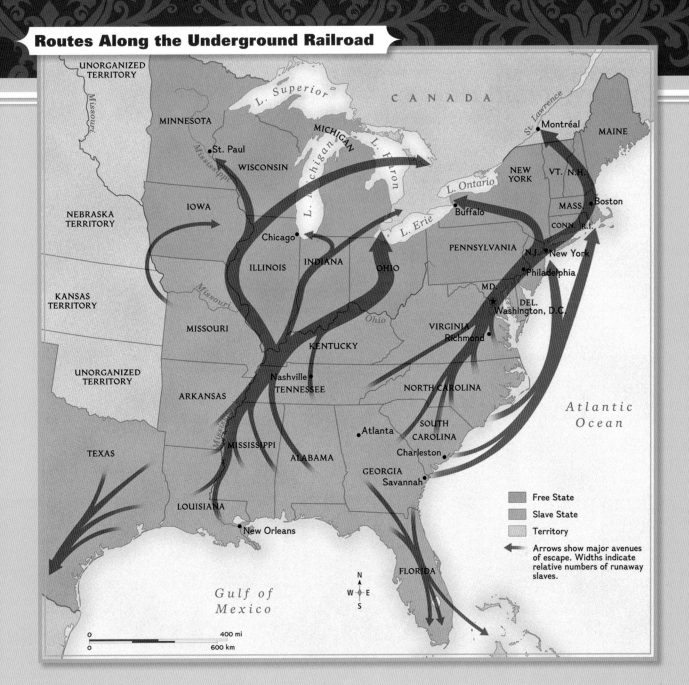

UNORGANIZED TERRITORY

L. Superior

CANADA

MINNESOTA

MICHIGAN

St. Lawrence

Montréal

MAINE

St. Paul

WISCONSIN

L. Michigan

L. Huron

NEW YORK

VT. N.H.

IOWA

L. Ontario

Boston

NEBRASKA TERRITORY

Chicago

L. Erie

Buffalo

MASS.

CONN. R.I.

ILLINOIS

INDIANA

OHIO

PENNSYLVANIA

N.J. New York

Philadelphia

KANSAS TERRITORY

Missouri

MISSOURI

MD.

DEL.

Washington, D.C.

KENTUCKY

VIRGINIA

Richmond

Ohio

UNORGANIZED TERRITORY

Nashville

TENNESSEE

NORTH CAROLINA

ARKANSAS

Atlanta

SOUTH CAROLINA

TEXAS

MISSISSIPPI

ALABAMA

Charleston

GEORGIA

Savannah

Atlantic Ocean

LOUISIANA

New Orleans

FLORIDA

Gulf of Mexico

N
W E
S

0   400 mi
0   600 km

Free State

Slave State

Territory

Arrows show major avenues of escape. Widths indicate relative numbers of runaway slaves.

Some runaways traveled through Texas to Mexico, where **slavery** was **illegal**. Others **fled** by boat to the islands of the Caribbean. Most followed the Underground Railroad to northern states or Canada, where slavery was also outlawed.

illegal not allowed by **law**
fled left

▶ **Before You Continue**

1. **Explain** Was a conductor's job on the Underground Railroad dangerous? Explain.

2. **Use Text Features** Why do the arrows on the map point both north and south?

Underground Heroes

Who were the heroes of the Underground Railroad? They were ordinary people. Some were formerly enslaved people who were freed or had **escaped**. Some belonged to religious groups. Some were from the North, and others were from the South. The members of the Underground Railroad had different reasons for helping people escape **slavery**. Yet they all shared the belief that people should not have to live in slavery.

Helping people escape was dangerous work. According to the **law**, people could be punished for **aiding** an enslaved person. The greatest danger, however, was from supporters of slavery. They sometimes **injured** or killed people who helped enslaved people escape.

▲ These twenty men were **arrested** for helping just one enslaved person **escape**.

aiding helping
injured hurt
arrested put in jail

◀ Rhoda Jones was a member of the Underground Railroad in Ohio.

The Gift of Freedom

Members of the Underground Railroad knew the work was dangerous, but they **accepted** the risks. Rhoda Jones was one example. She lived in Ohio. Some people in that state had been killed for their work on the Underground Railroad. Still, Jones opened her home to people **escaping slavery**.

Rhoda Jones was just one of the thousands who **risked** great danger to help others. The members of the Underground Railroad didn't get money for their work. Most never became famous. Yet they were all willing to put their lives at risk to help others find **freedom**. ❖

accepted took

▶ **Before You Continue**

1. **Paraphrase** In your own words, explain what kinds of people belonged to the Underground Railroad.
2. **Make Inferences** How do you think those people felt about their work?

Key Words

abolish	law
distinguish	plantation
emancipation	risk
equality	route
escape	slavery
freedom	

Compare Figurative Language

Authors use **figurative language**, such as similes or metaphors, to help you to create pictures in your mind. The pictures help you see, hear, feel, and understand what the authors are writing about.

Work with a partner. Find figurative language from the selection to complete the chart below.

Comparison Chart

"Journey to Freedom"	"Crossing Bok Chitto"
Enslaved people who were running away often traveled hundreds of miles to **reach** freedom.	**Quick as a bird**, Little Mo flew across the stones.
In my mind, I can *see the* people arriving at a *safe place*.	In my mind, I can *see Little Mo* hopping quickly across the *stones.*

Talk Together

Both selections talk about what people **risked** to help others find justice and **freedom** . How does each author use figurative language to make the people and events come to life? Use **Key Words** to talk about your ideas.

Present Tense Action Verbs

A **present tense action verb** tells about an action that is happening now. The verb must agree with the subject.

Grammar Rules Present Tense Action Verbs	
• Use **-s** at the end of an action verb if the subject is **he**, **she**, or **it**. he she it	Duncan learn**s** about slavery. **He** learn**s** about slavery. Peggy visit**s** a plantation. **She** visit**s** a plantation. History remind**s** us about our past. **It** remind**s** us about our past.
• Do not use **-s** for **I**, **you**, **we**, or **they**.	**I** write about history. **You** listen to the speech. **We** learn about Civil Rights struggles. **They** read about women's rights.

Read Present Tense Action Verbs

Read the passage. Work with a partner to find present tense action verbs.

> Every Sunday morning, Martha Tom crosses Bok Chitto. She sits with Little Mo's family in church. She sings the songs in English, and then she sings them in Choctaw on her way home.

Write Present Tense Action Verbs

Look at the illustrations on pages 236–237. Write two sentences that describe what you see. Use a present tense action verb in each sentence. Be sure the subject and verb agree. Compare your sentences with a partner's.

Language Frames

• I want _____ .
• You want _____ .
• How about _____ ?

Negotiate

Listen to Carmen and Rachel's song. Then use **Language Frames** to talk to a partner about ways to achieve justice through negotiation.

THE MURAL

Song

Carmen: Let's discuss the school mural.

Rachel: Yes. The problem is clear.

I want to paint lots of animals.

You want to paint the best school volunteers.

Carmen: Maybe we could put them together—

There's no need for regrets.

How about we paint volunteers

with their favorite pets?

Tune: "Take Me Out to the Ballgame"

Key Words

Key Words
conditions
demands
labor
nonviolence
protest
strike

🔊 Key Words

Look at these photographs. Use **Key Words** to talk about how some workers **protest** unfair treatment.

striker

Workers go on strike. A **strike** is a way to protest with **nonviolence**.

Workers often strike for better **labor**, or work, **conditions**.

demands

Strikers make signs to express their **demands**.

Talk Together

How can you achieve justice through nonviolence? With a partner, use the **Key Words** and Language Frames from page 256 to discuss the question.

Thinking Map

Sequence

When events happen in a certain order, they happen in **sequence**.
When you think about sequence, use:

- time order words, such as *first*, *next*, *then*, *finally*.

- names of days, months, and seasons.

Look at these pictures of Carmen and Rachel.

Map and Talk

You can make a sequence chain to show the order of events. Here's
how you make one.

Each event goes in a box in the sequence chain. The first event goes in
the first box. The second event goes in the second box, and so on.

Sequence Chain

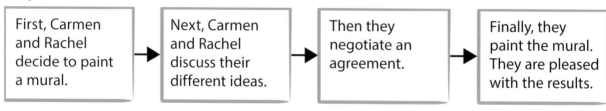

First, Carmen and Rachel decide to paint a mural. → Next, Carmen and Rachel discuss their different ideas. → Then they negotiate an agreement. → Finally, they paint the mural. They are pleased with the results.

Use a sequence chain to tell about something you negotiated. Tell the
events in time order while a partner makes a sequence chain.

More Key Words

Use these words to talk about "The Troublemaker: The Story of Nelson Mandela" and "Sisters Fighting for the Oceans."

barrier
noun

A **barrier** prevents you from getting to something. The wall was a **barrier** to freedom.

conflict
noun

A **conflict** is a disagreement between people or groups.

demonstrate
verb

When you **demonstrate** something, you show or express your feelings or knowledge about it.

oppose
verb

Oppose means to disagree with an idea or action. They protested to **oppose** the government's decision.

require
verb

Require means to need. A plant **requires** sunlight to survive.

Talk Together

Work with a partner. Make an **Expanded Meaning Map** for each **Key Word**.

Expanded Meaning Map

┌ What the Word Means ┐
disagreement

Word
conflict

┌ Examples ┐ ┌ What It Is Like ┐
argument, quarrel difficult, uncomfortable

259

Learn to Make Inferences

Look at the cartoon. The caption does not say why the women are **demonstrating**. You can use what you see and what you already know to figure out, or **make an inference** about, what the women are **protesting**.

Protest in front of Atti's Movers

When you read, you can **make inferences**, too.

How to Make Inferences

	1. Look for details in the text.	I read _____.
	2. Think about what you already know about the details and the topic.	I know _____.
	3. Put your ideas together. What else can you figure out about the text?	And so _____.

Talk Together

Read Carmen's editorial for the school newspaper. Read the sample inference. Then use **Language Frames** to make inferences. Tell a partner about them.

Editorial

Peaceful Protest—It Works!

Today I learned that peaceful protest works. A week ago, I noticed a group of women workers marching outside Atti's Movers. They were **protesting** because they **opposed** the fact that they did not have the same rights as male workers. They wanted to break the **barriers** between men and women on the job. They wanted equal pay for equal time. One of the signs they carried read, "We **Require** Equal Pay for Equal Work!"

This morning, I spotted an Atti's moving van across the street. New neighbors were moving in. I also noticed that the movers were both men and women. They seemed to be laughing and joking with each other.

I could tell that the **conflict** was over. The **strike** had been a success. The women presented their **demands**, and Atti's Movers heard them.

This **demonstrates** that peaceful protest, or **nonviolence**, is a great way for getting results! We should remember that through peaceful negotiation, anything is possible.

> "I read that the women wanted equal pay.
>
> I know that when people protest they want to change something.
>
> And so the women must be earning less than the men."

◄ = a good place to stop and make an inference

261

Read a Biography

Genre

A **biography** is the story of a person's life, written by another person. Dates and words such as *then*, *finally*, and *later* tell you when events happen.

Point of View

Point of view describes how a story is told. In the third-person point of view, a narrator outside the story tells it. When the third-person point of view is *limited*, the narrator does not know everything. Instead, the narrator may know what only one character thinks and feels.

So Nelson went to live with his uncle, his aunt, and his cousin, Justice. The boys soon became as close as brothers and did everything together. But Nelson never forgot his uncle's words. He wanted to honor his father's wishes, so he studied as hard as he could.

The Troublemaker

The Story of Nelson Mandela

by **Penelope McKimm**

Find out how events in Nelson
Mandela's childhood helped him
become a fighter for justice.

Rolihlahla. Madiba. Tata. Khulu. Dalibhunga. He had many
names, with many different meanings, but most of us know
him by his English name: Nelson, the name given to him by his
teacher when he was just seven years old.

Nelson Mandela is known and loved all over the world
as a great leader and a wise and peaceful **warrior**. In his own
country of South Africa, he is called Tata (father) or Khulu (the
Great One). His words and wisdom have brought comfort and
inspiration to millions of people. He is an example for those
who struggle for justice, and his story shows us the power
of **nonviolence**, **persistence**, and hope—a hope so powerful
that years spent in prison could not **crush** his spirit.

▲ January 1994, President Nelson
Mandela waves to supporters in
South Africa as he campaigns for
presidential election.

warrior fighter
persistence not giving up
crush destroy

Rolihlahla was born in the village of Mvezo, which lies in a beautiful valley alongside the Mbhashe River. The village belonged to the Thembu people. They kept animals, mostly **cattle** and sheep. As a small boy, Rolihlahla helped his father care for the family's animals. When he had finished for the day, he would play with the other boys in the village. One of their favorite games was soccer. They also practiced fighting with sticks, pretending to be great warriors from generations past.

In the Xhosa language, Rolihlahla's name means "**troublemaker**." Could this have been part of the reason why his fight for justice as a grown-up got him into so much trouble?

cattle cows and bulls
troublemaker person who causes problems

▲ **Xhosa huts in the village of Mvezo**

Rolihlahla's father was an important member of the Thembu tribe. As the son of an elder, Rolihlahla was allowed to sit and listen to the **councils** of the **chiefs** as they discussed matters of importance. Once their discussions were over, they would tell stories, and Rolihlahla learned of his tribe's history. He learned about what life had been like before Europeans came to Africa and how the African people had fought bravely against them.

When Rolihlahla was still very small, his father and other members of the Thembu tribe were forced to leave Mvezo by a white **magistrate**. Although he was still very young when it happened, Rolihlahla never forgot the shock and pain his family felt as they left their village behind or the injustice of the magistrate's decision.

▲ Nelson Mandela grew up as part of the Thembu tribe in South Africa.

councils meetings
chiefs tribal leaders
magistrate judge

Rolihlahla and his family moved to the village of Qunu. Once he began to **recover from** the shock and sadness of the move, Rolihlahla was able to enjoy a happy childhood in the village. He still helped his father with the family's animals, but he also swam in the river and played with the other children.

There was a small school in Qunu, and Rolihlahla started attending when he was seven years old. In those days, schoolteachers followed a tradition of giving English names to all new students. His teacher was a kind woman called Miss Mdingane.

"Your name is Nelson," she told him.

▲ Rolihlahla's schoolteacher in Qunu gave him the English name, Nelson.

recover from overcome, feel better about

▶ **Before You Continue**

1. **Compare/Contrast** What changes happened in Nelson Mandela's life before he was seven years old?
2. **Point of View** Does the narrator of this story know what all the characters think and feel? How do you know?

267

▶ **Predict**
How will Nelson become
involved in the struggle for justice
in South Africa?

Nelson's father died in 1930, when Nelson was twelve years old. Nelson's uncle, who was also a Thembu chief, came to see him.

"Your father and I had an agreement," he told Nelson, "that if anything ever happened to him, I was to take care of you. You are coming to live with me. I will send you to school. It was very important to your father that you receive a good education."

So Nelson went to live with his uncle, his aunt, and his cousin, Justice. The boys soon became as close as brothers and did everything together. But Nelson never forgot his uncle's words. He wanted to honor his father's wishes, so he studied as hard as he could. Most universities in South Africa were adopting a "whites-only" policy. However, when he graduated from high school, he was accepted into Fort Hare College, a **reputable** university that accepted students of all races.

▲ **Fort Hare College, South Africa, circa 1930**

reputable good

While at university, Nelson became interested in law and politics, deciding that the best way to help his people would be to become a lawyer. If he were a lawyer, he would be able to defend people facing injustice and help them fight for their rights.

Nelson joined a student group called the Students' Representative Council, which was trying to improve the living **conditions** of students at the university. After the university ignored the students' **demands**, the group organized a protest. Many students who participated in the **strike** were **expelled**, including Nelson.

expelled made to leave the university

▲ **Students at Fort Hare College organized a protest to try to improve student living conditions.**

But this didn't stop him. In 1941, Nelson moved to Johannesburg. He got a job as a security guard at a mine and was horrified by the **conditions** of the black miners. They were forced to work long hours and live far from their families. They were paid very little and did not have holidays. If they tried to **quit**, they were often put in jail.

Nelson and his friend Oliver Tambo went into business together. They wanted to use their business to help people. The two men worked very hard to assist other black Africans who were facing injustice. They helped families who were being forced to leave their homes, workers who had lost their jobs unfairly, and other people who were suffering because of racism in South Africa.

▲ **Nelson Mandela and Oliver Tambo, December 6, 1990**

quit leave their job

▲ Under the apartheid laws, black, mixed-race, and Asian South Africans needed a pass to travel.

In 1948, the South African government **enacted** a set of laws called the apartheid laws. These laws ensured that only white South Africans would have power, freedom, and opportunities for a good life. All other South Africans—those who were black, mixed race, and Asian—were forced to live as **second-class citizens**. They were not allowed to vote in elections or run for office. They were excluded from well-paid jobs and good schools. They were forced to live in certain areas without running water or electricity.

The apartheid laws also introduced a system of **curfews**, meaning that no one, except white South Africans, was allowed to be out after dark. To be able to travel anywhere, even short distances, black, mixed-race, and Asian South Africans needed a pass. If the police caught them without their passes, they could be arrested.

enacted started using
second-class citizens people without rights
curfews rules stating that everyone must stay at home between particular times

▶ **Before You Continue**

1. **Clarify** In what ways did the apartheid laws worsen injustice in South Africa?
2. **Make Inferences** What **barriers** do you think Nelson and Oliver faced when starting their business?

▶ **Predict**
How will Nelson Mandela fight
against the racist apartheid laws?

Nelson and many of his friends joined the African National Congress, which was a group that used **nonviolence** to **protest** the injustice of the apartheid laws.

On one such occasion, Nelson and about fifty others marched into an area of Johannesburg that was reserved for whites. This activity was against the apartheid laws, and they were arrested. In other parts of Africa, large groups of black, mixed-race, and Asian South Africans entered other "whites-only" public spaces, sat on "whites-only" benches, and went into the streets after curfew.

Although most of the protesters were quickly **released**, the large number of arrests began to **overwhelm** the police and the courts—which was the protesters' intention. They wanted to show that the laws not only were unfair but also could not be made to work.

Many people **protested** against the ▲
injustice of the apartheid laws.

released let out of jail
overwhelm be too much for

The Campaign involved many different kinds of nonviolent actions. Apart from **strikes**, one important action was the **bus boycott**. People refused to pay money for a service that was treating them unfairly. During the bus boycott, thousands of people, mostly black South Africans, would walk for hours instead of taking the bus to show **opposition** to the high cost of transport and low wages for black workers. Sometimes white South Africans, who were allowed to drive cars, would stop and offer them rides.

At first, white officials in the South African government did not believe that the African National Congress or the Campaign would last long or be successful. But, the protests were **drawing** attention from other countries and the movement was becoming more popular, even among some white South Africans.

bus boycott staying away from using city busses

drawing getting

political prisoners people who have been put in prison for opposing the government

▲ Police arrest students who held an anti-apartheid demonstration to release **political prisoners**.

In 1956, the South African government accused Nelson and several other members of the African National Congress of **treason**. They spent five years fighting the charges before they were finally **cleared**. Over the next few years, Nelson and his friends would be arrested several more times. But Nelson was determined to fight for justice. He remembered the stories of his ancestors who had defended their land and the pain his family had suffered when they were made to leave their village. Giving up his fight would be **unthinkable**.

In 1960, Nelson and several other members of the African National Congress were arrested again, accused of planning to overthrow the government. For a while, it looked like Nelson would be sentenced to death. Instead, he and his friends were sentenced to life in prison.

▲ October 13, 1958
Nelson Mandela outside court in
Pretoria, South Africa where he was
on trial for treason

treason betraying their country
cleared found innocent
unthinkable impossible

Nelson was in prison for 27 years. In the beginning, Nelson and his companions were **forbidden from** reading newspapers or books, or from having any contact with the outside world. Prison was a cruel, cold place, but Nelson was clever at finding ways to save his hope and that of his companions.

The prisoners were made to work hard making building materials, and Nelson encouraged his fellow prisoners to **rebel** by working very slowly. At first, the prison authorities ignored this protest, but the prisoners persisted until they were finally allowed some improvements in their living conditions.

Nelson learned Afrikaans, the language spoken by many white South Africans. When he began to speak with the prison guards in their own language, they could not help admiring him. They became sympathetic with their **charismatic** prisoner and gave him newspapers and books, and even helped him see his baby granddaughter!

▲ **Nelson Mandela in his cell where he had been imprisoned for 27 years**

forbidden from not allowed to
rebel fight back
charismatic likeable

▶ **Before You Continue**

1. **Clarify** How did Nelson find ways to stay hopeful while in prison?
2. **Make Inferences** How did learning Afrikaans help Nelson make friends with the guards?

▶ **Predict**
What will happen after Nelson
is released from prison?

N elson was known as the "world's most famous prisoner."
After he was sent to prison, people all over the world began
to **protest** . They sent letters to the government of South
Africa demanding the release of Nelson and an end to the
apartheid laws.

Twice, the South African
government offered to release
Nelson if he promised to **abandon**
his fight against apartheid. But
Nelson did not agree. For him, the
only acceptable solution was an end
to the apartheid laws.

Then, a new government
was elected in South Africa. This
government offered to release
Nelson and his companions and to
work with him on developing a new
constitution that would give equal
rights to all South Africans. In 1990,
Nelson and his companions walked
out of the prison to see thousands of
people cheering.

Nelson Mandela with his wife Winnie after ▲
being released from prison in 1990

abandon stop

▲ A mural in Soweto, Johannesburg, showing former South African President, Nelson Mandela, during different times in his life

Nelson Mandela was no longer a prisoner, but his fight was far from over. The African National Congress elected Nelson as its president, and along with the President of South Africa, F. W. de Klerk, he began the long and difficult **task** of building a new country, where all people could enjoy equal rights and opportunities.

In 1994, South Africa had its first truly **democratic** elections, in which all South Africans, including those excluded under the old apartheid laws, were allowed to vote. Nelson was elected president of South Africa. As president, he worked very hard to achieve peace.

Incredibly, and in spite of his long suffering, Nelson lived the rest of his life spreading a message of forgiveness and hope.

"As I walked out the door toward the gate that would lead to my freedom," he said, "I knew if I didn't leave my **bitterness** and hatred behind, I'd still be in prison." ❖

task work
democratic free and fair
bitterness anger

▶ **Before You Continue**

1. **Clarify** What were the events that finally led to Nelson's release from prison?

2. **Make Inferences** What do you think Nelson means when he says, "I'd still be in prison?"

Think and Respond

Key Words	
barrier	nonviolence
conditions	oppose
conflict	protest
demands	require
demonstrate	strike
labor	

Talk About It

1. What are the most important events in the **biography** of Nelson Mandela? How does the author lead up to these events?

2. Imagine that you are Nelson Mandela, talking with the South African government as they build a new constitution. Use **Language Frames** to **negotiate** some new laws for the country.

3. Compare Nelson's life in Johannesburg to his childhood in the village.

   In his village, _____. In Johannesburg, _____.

Write About It

Imagine that a statue of Nelson Mandela is to be built in your community. You have been asked to make a sign for the statue. Write three sentences to put on the sign. Use **Key Words** to explain why Nelson Mandela is a hero.

> **Nelson Mandela is a hero because** _____.
> **He showed us that** _____.

Sequence

Use the sequence chain to show what happened in "The Troublemaker."
In your own words, write the events in the order that they happened.

Sequence Chain

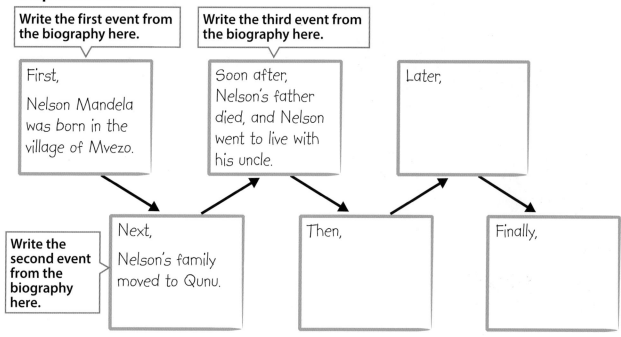

Write the first event from the biography here.

Write the third event from the biography here.

First,
Nelson Mandela was born in the village of Mvezo.

Soon after, Nelson's father died, and Nelson went to live with his uncle.

Later,

Write the second event from the biography here.

Next,
Nelson's family moved to Qunu.

Then,

Finally,

Now use your sequence chain as you retell the biography to a partner. Tell the events in the order that they happened. Use **Key Words**.

First, _____ . Next, _____ . Soon after, _____ . Then, _____ . Finally, _____ .

Fluency

Practice reading with phrasing. Rate your reading.

How did Nelson Mandela achieve justice? Draw a picture of people today who are working for justice. Write a caption for your picture. Use **Key Words**. Share your picture with the class.

279

Synonyms

Synonyms are words that have the same, or nearly the same, meaning, such as *hard* and *difficult*. One word can have several synonyms. What words describe this picture?

support

help   **aid**

assist

Sometimes synonyms are used in analogies. Identifying synonyms can help you figure out analogies. Look at these analogies.

[<u>help</u> is to <u>assist</u>] as [<u>aid</u> is to <u>support</u>]

Try It Together

Read each item. Choose the word that best completes the analogy.

1. **barrier is to obstacle as problem is to** _____

   A solution

   B dilemma

   C argue

   D procedure

2. **Quiet is to silent as noisy is to** _____

   A sound

   B loud

   C outrageous

   D easy

Sisters Fighting for the Oceans

by Penelope McKimm

Melati and Isabel Wijsen started a **campaign** to reduce plastic in the oceans.

What Is Environmental Justice?

Environmental justice is the idea that every person has a right to a healthy environment, including clean air, clean water, and healthy oceans. Environmental injustice occurs when people are **excluded from** decisions that affect their environment and, therefore, their lives. People who suffer the most because of environmental damage live in the poorest, most **vulnerable** communities.

Melati and Isabel Wijsen are two sisters fighting for environmental justice on the island of Bali. When they were just 10 and 12 years old, they started a **campaign** to reduce plastic waste in Bali and all over the world.

excluded from left out of
vulnerable defenseless
campaign movement

▶ **Before You Continue**

1. **Clarify** What does environmental justice mean? Can you think of an example from your own country?
2. **Make Inferences** How is Melati and Isabel's campaign related to environmental justice?

▲ Bali's beaches are disappearing under a mountain of garbage.

▲ Fish and other animals eat the plastic and die.

Bali: Green Paradise or Paradise Lost?

Bali, the island in Indonesia where Melati and Isabel were born, is famous for its beautiful mountains, forests, and beaches. Millions of tourists visit the island every year. Melati calls it "a green **paradise**."

But Bali also has a problem with plastic garbage. The island produces enough plastic every day to fill a 14-story building. The plastic goes into Bali's rivers and then into the ocean. Every year, during the **wet season**, thousands of tons of plastic garbage are washed up on Bali's beaches. Thousands of birds and other animals eat the plastic and die. And it affects people, too, because fish and seafood also become **contaminated** with plastic.

paradise place of beauty
wet season rainiest time of the year
contaminated polluted

Diana, Princess of Wales, a key volunteer of the British Red Cross Landmine Campaign

An Inspirational Lesson

One day, Melati and Isabel's schoolteacher taught them about **significant** people from history, including Nelson Mandela, Princess Diana, and Mahatma Gandhi. They wanted to be significant, too, but they did not want to wait until they were grown up to make a difference. They sat down together and **brainstormed** problems Bali was facing. They realized that plastic garbage was a serious problem, but also one that could be solved.

Because Bali produces so much plastic garbage, it made sense for Melati and Isabel to **focus** on reducing the number of plastic bags as a **realistic** goal.

▲ Nelson Mandela, South African activist and former president

significant important
brainstormed made a list of ideas
focus concentrate
realistic possible

▶ **Before You Continue**

1. **Clarify** Where did Melati and Isabel get the idea to start their campaign?
2. **Make Inferences** What do you think Melati and Isabel's school was like?

Building a Movement

The first step the sisters took was to find out more about the problem. The more they learned, the more they realized that plastic bags were simply not useful enough to **justify** the damage they caused. They also learned about **efforts** to ban plastic bags in other countries and cities around the world.

They knew they would not be able to achieve their goal on their own. They asked their teachers, parents, and friends for help. They went to other schools on the island to talk about their idea and they met with the mayor of their village, who agreed to help them as much as he could.

justify make acceptable
efforts work

First Successes

Melati and Isabel organized a **beach cleanup**, and more than 12,000 volunteers came to help. Working with other communities in Bali, they started **distributing** bags made from materials other than plastic, such as recycled newspaper and net.

When the governor of Bali ignored their request to ban plastic bags on the island, they decided to start a petition. After knocking on many doors, they convinced the manager of the Ngurah Rai International Airport in Bali to let them talk to people in the airport's customs and immigration area. By doing this, they got more than 100,000 people to **sign** their petition!

Melati and Isabel learned that more than 16 million people arrive and depart from the Bali airport every year.

beach cleanup event to remove garbage from the beach

distributing giving out

sign write your name

▶ **Before You Continue**

1. **Make Inferences** What do you think a petition is? How do you think it works?

2. **Figurative Language** Can you think of a different way to say "knocking on many doors?"

Taking Risks

Melati and Isabel asked for a **hearing** with the governor of Bali to talk about their idea to ban plastic bags on the island. But the governor would not agree to a meeting. The sisters felt **frustrated**.

Then, they were invited to go to India to talk about their campaign. They visited the house where Mahatma Gandhi had lived, and they learned that he had used **hunger strikes** as a form of nonviolent protest. When they returned to Bali, they had news for their parents.

"We're going on a hunger strike!" they told them.

Mahatma Gandhi used hunger strikes as a form of **nonviolent protest** during India's struggle for Independence from Great Britain. ▶

▲ Because they were very young, Melati and Isabel had to be supervised by a dietitian during their hunger **strike**.

hearing meeting
frustrated stuck
hunger strikes refusal to eat
nonviolent protest a demonstration without violence

Victory!

When the governor heard about Melati and Isabel's hunger **strike**, he became worried. He sent police to their school, and the police took the sisters to see him at his **residence**. He gave the sisters a letter, promising to ban plastic bags in Bali within a few years.

The sisters met with the governor several times to make sure he was keeping his promises. Later, they were invited to speak at the United Nations for World Oceans Day. Now their organization, *Bye Bye Plastic Bags*, has **chapters** all over the world.

"We've learned kids can do things. We can make things happen," says Melati. ❖

▲ **Bali was declared free of plastic bags in 2018, and the government of Indonesia has committed to banning plastic bags by the year 2021.**

residence home
chapters groups

▶ **Before You Continue**

1. **Make Inferences** What risks did Melati and Isabel take to make the governor listen to them?
2. **Make Connections** Melati and Isabel were inspired by Nelson Mandela's story. How did they follow his example in their own campaign?

Key Words	
barrier	nonviolence
conditions	oppose
conflict	protest
demands	require
demonstrate	strike
labor	

Compare Literary Language

Different kinds of texts have different narrative styles. "Sisters Fighting for the Oceans" is written in the style of a report.

A report uses **facts** and **information** to help us understand something.

"The Troublemaker" is written in the style of creative non-fiction. Creative non-fiction also gives us facts and information, but often uses literary devices, such as **imagery** and **foreshadowing**, to communicate with readers in a special way.

- **Imagery** helps readers imagine how people, places or things look, sound, smell, taste, or feel.

- **Foreshadowing** gives clues at the beginning of the text that gets readers interested to find out what will happen at the end.

Work with a partner to complete the chart.

Comparison Chart

	"The Troublemaker"	"Sisters Fighting for the Oceans"
Facts and information	p. 275 _____	p. 282 The island produces enough plastic every day to fill a 14-story building.
Foreshadowing	p. 265 Rolihlahla's name means "troublemaker." Could this have been the reason why his fight for justice got him into so much trouble?	
Imagery	p. 265 _____	p. 282 _____

Talk Together

How does each biography help you understand how childhood can affect a person's ideas about justice? Use **Key Words** to discuss your ideas.

Forms of Be and Have

The verbs **be** and **have** use special forms. Each verb must agree with its subject. You can write some subjects and verbs as contractions. A contraction is a short way of writing two words as one word.

Grammar Rules — Forms of Be and Have

	Forms of **Be**	Forms of **Have**
• For **I**, use	I **am** or **I'm**	I **have** or **I've**
• For **you**, use	you **are** or **you're**	you **have** or **you've**
• For **he, she, it**, use	she **is** or **she's** he **is** or **he's** it **is** or **it's**	she **has** or **she's** he **has** or **he's** it **has** or **it's**
• For **we**, use	we **are** or **we're**	we **have** or **we've**
• For **they**, use	they **are** or **they're**	they **have** or **they've**

Read Forms of Be and Have

Read the passage about Melati and Isabel Wijsen. What forms of **be** and **have** can you find? Tell a partner when they are used as helping verbs.

> Bali, the island in Indonesia where Melati and Isabel were born, is famous for its beautiful mountains, forests, and beaches. Millions of tourists visit the island every year. Melati calls it "a green paradise." But Bali also has a problem with plastic garbage.

Write Forms of Be and Have

Look at the photos on pages 284–285. Write two sentences about them. Use the verb **be** or **have** in each sentence. Be sure the subject and verb agree. Compare your sentences with a partner's.

Write As a Researcher

Write a Research Report ✏️

Write a report about an event in history when justice was achieved. Place your reports in a journal called *Justice in the World*.

Study a Model

For a research report, you gather information from several sources. You think about what you've learned and decide what it all means.

Read William's report about a famous fight for civil rights justice.

The title and introduction capture the reader's interest.

A Bus Ride to Justice
William Brown

In 1955, an African-American woman named Rosa Parks refused to give up her seat on the bus to a Caucasian. She was arrested for this "crime." The event led to a famous protest: the Montgomery Bus Boycott. **The boycott showed that people could fight for justice without using violence** .

A **statement of the main idea** tells what the writer will try to prove in his report.

Each paragraph has a topic sentence that supports the main idea. The writer supports each main idea with evidence.

In the early 1950s, the bus system in Montgomery, Alabama, was segregated. African Americans had to sit at the back of the bus. They also had to give up their seats if the Caucasian section filled up. This is what Rosa Parks refused to do.

Rosa Parks' arrest angered African-American leaders. They asked African Americans to refuse to ride the city buses.

The paper has a clear organization. Events are presented in the sequence in which they happened.

A group was organized to handle the boycott. They asked a new young minister, Dr. Martin Luther King, Jr., to lead the group. He agreed.

Quotation marks show a **direct quotation**.

King insisted that the boycott be kept peaceful. He said, **"We are not here advocating violence."** He showed people that they could fight back without breaking any laws.

Thousands of African Americans boycotted the buses for over a year. Eventually the protest was successful. In 1956, the United States Supreme Court ordered Montgomery to provide integrated seating on public buses.

Sources

A final page lists the sources William used for the report.

Delano, Marfé Ferguson. "American Heroes." Washington, D.C: National Geographic Society, 2005.

"King, Martin Luther, Jr." World Book Encyclopedia. 2009. Print.

Dove, Rita. "The Time 100: Rosa Parks." Time, Inc., 20 Nov. 2009. Web.15 Feb. 2010. http://www.time.com/time/time100/heroes/profile/parks01.html

Prewrite

1. **Choose a Topic** What is justice? What examples can you find from the past? Work with a partner to brainstorm and discuss ideas. Narrow your topic to one that you can cover well in a short report.

2. **List Your Research Questions** What do you already know about your topic? What do you want to find out? Write questions you could use to guide your research.

Research Questions

- Why did the Montgomery Bus Boycott happen?
- Where did it take place?
- Who participated in the boycott?
- How were the buses segregated?
- What did city officials do?

---

3. **Create a Research Plan** A research report must contain information from several sources. Your research plan contains your topic and your ideas about the sources you can use to answer them. There are two main types of sources, **primary sources** and **secondary sources**.

Topic: The Montgomery Bus Boycott

Primary Sources	Secondary Sources
* Rosa Parks' journal or diary	* books about the Montgomery Bus Boycott
* letters written by people who participated in the boycott	* online articles about Rosa Parks and the bus boycott
* arrest documents	* encyclopedia entry about the Montgomery Bus Boycott

---

Primary sources, such as letters, diaries, and official documents, provide direct, firsthand knowledge from eyewitnesses to the event.

Secondary sources give information based on primary sources. They include nonfiction books, newspapers, and websites.

Gather Information

1. **Identify Sources** Valid, or reliable, sources are up to date. They are written by a group or person who is an expert in the area. Skim the source to see if it has the information you need.

2. **Create source cards** Use index cards to record important information about each source you use. Give each card a number.

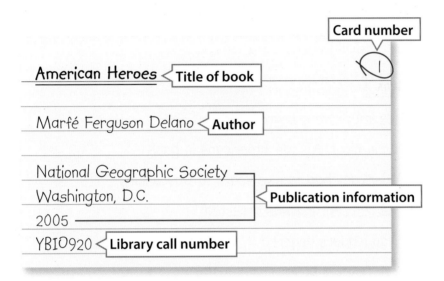

3. **Make Note Cards** Record important ideas on note cards. Paraphrase, or put all of the information in your own words. Use quotation marks for anything you pick up word for word.

   Try to use some visuals in your report. Keep a separate file for any pictures, maps, or charts you may want to use.

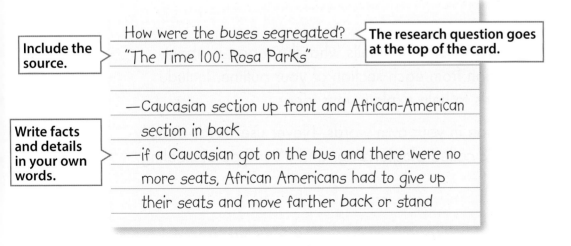

Get Organized

1. **Sort Your Cards** Use the research questions at the top of your cards to put them into groups. Put the groups in an order that would make sense to your reader.

2. **Organize Your Details** Use an outline or other graphic organizer to help you. Each group, or category, from your cards becomes a main idea. The details from each card support the main ideas.

Outline

Use Roman numerals for main ideas.

Use capital letters for supporting points. There must always be at least an A and a B.

Add more details using Arabic numbers (1, 2, 3).

I. Buses in Montgomery were segregated

   A. Caucasians in front, African Americans in back

   B. African-Americans had to give seats to Caucasians

   C. Rosa Parks refused and was arrested

II. African-American leaders angered

   A. Made plan to boycott buses

   B. Formed group to organize boycott

     1. Elected Martin Luther King, Jr. as leader

     2. Agreed boycott would be peaceful

Draft

- Write an interesting introduction that tells what the report is about. Then, write a paragraph from each section of your outline. Include maps, photos, or charts to help explain your ideas.

- Write all the information in your own words. Never use words directly from the source. This is called **plagiarizing**, and it's a type of stealing.

Revise

1. **Read, Retell, Respond** Read your draft aloud to a partner. Next, talk about ways to improve your writing.

2. **Make Changes** Think about your draft and your partner's suggestions. Use revision marks to make your changes.

   - Have you put everything in your own words? If not, think of a new way to present the information.

     > He showed people that they could fight back without breaking any laws. ~~Instead, he encouraged people to use legal protest as their main weapon.~~

   - Are your facts presented in a logical order that your readers can follow? Move any that seem out of place.

     > Eventually the protest was successful. ~~That was after~~ thousands of African Americans boycotted the buses for over a year.

Edit and Proofread

Carefully check all your facts, as well as names, dates, and numbers. Make sure direct quotes are in quotation marks.

Present

1. **Make a Final Copy** Make a final copy of your research report. Ask your teacher if there is a special format, or way of presenting your report, that you should use. Add a source list at the end.

2. **Share With Others** Present your paper as an oral report or multimedia slideshow. Then, with your classmates, collect your reports and put them in a book called *Justice in the World*.

Talk Together

In this unit, you found lots of answers to the **Big Question**. Now use your concept map to discuss the **Big Question** with the class.

Concept Map

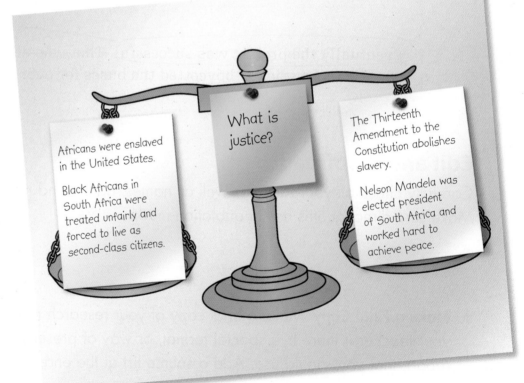

Make a Poster

Make a poster about justice. Use your concept map to help you.

Share Your Ideas

Choose one of these ways to share your ideas about the **Big Question**.

Write It!

Make a Collage

Make a collage of headlines that have to do with justice. Look in magazines and newspapers. Cut out the headlines and glue them on a sheet of paper. Cut out or draw a picture to go with the headlines.

Talk About It!

Hold a Debate

With a small group, hold a debate. Choose an issue people are talking about now in your school or community. Write arguments for and against the issue on index cards. Use the cards to help you make your points.

Do It!

Research Protest Songs

Work in a group to research protest songs, or songs that shine a light on injustice. Collect several examples of protest songs, and put them together in a book. Write an introduction that tells about each song.

Talk About It!

Meet the Reporters

Role-play a press conference with the real people and the story characters in this unit. Have "reporters" ask questions about the fight for equal rights. The "freedom fighters" answer the questions by telling what they did to help people find freedom or win equal rights.

Picture Dictionary

The definitions are for the words as they are introduced in the selections of this book.

Parts of an Entry

The **entry** shows how the word is spelled.

The **picture** helps you understand more about the meaning of the word.

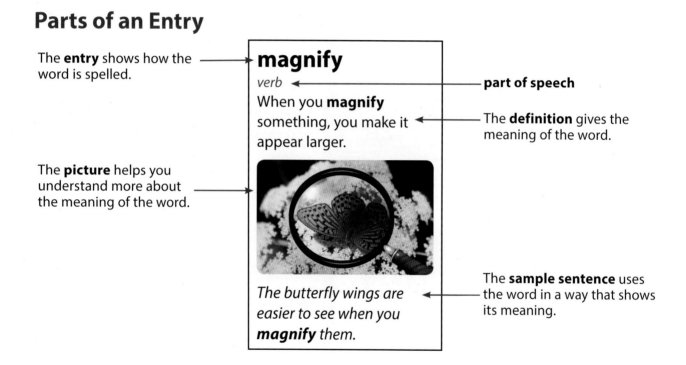

magnify

verb

When you **magnify** something, you make it appear larger.

The butterfly wings are easier to see when you **magnify** *them.*

part of speech

The **definition** gives the meaning of the word.

The **sample sentence** uses the word in a way that shows its meaning.

A

abolish
verb

When you officially end something, you **abolish** it.

*The scientist works to **abolish** disease.*

absorb
verb

When you take something in and hold it, you **absorb** it.

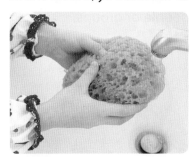

*The sponge **absorbs** the water.*

adapt
verb

If you **adapt**, you change.

*Visitors to Japan must **adapt** to a new way of eating.*

alternate
adjective

Alternate means different.

*He must find an **alternate** location.*

assume
verb

When you **assume** something, you think it is true without checking the facts.

*Don't **assume** you know the way. Check your map!*

B

barrier
noun

A **barrier** prevents you from getting to something.

*The wall was a **barrier** to freedom.*

C

carnivore
noun

A **carnivore** is an animal that eats other animals.

*A lion is a **carnivore**.*

challenge
noun

A **challenge** is a difficult task or situation.

*Carrying all the books at once is a **challenge**.*

chlorophyll
noun

Chlorophyll is the green part of plants that lets them use sunlight to help make their food.

***Chlorophyll** is what makes plants look green.*

a
b
c
d
e
f
g
h
i
j
k
l
m
n
o
p
q
r
s
t
u
v
w
x
y
z

a
b
c
d
e
f
g
h
i
j
k
l
m
n
o
p
q
r
s
t
u
v
w
x
y
z

circuit

noun

A **circuit** is the path that an electrical current will flow through.

*When electricity goes through the **circuit**, the light bulb turns on.*

citizenship

noun

Citizenship is belonging to a country. Citizenship also gives you the rights and duties of that country.

*Her **citizenship** makes her proud and happy.*

classify

verb

When you **classify** things, you put them into groups based on their similarities.

Amphibians

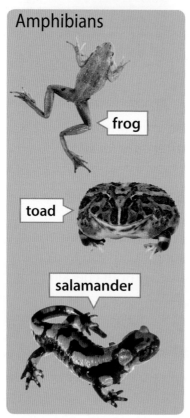

frog

toad

salamander

*You can **classify** frogs, toads, and salamanders as amphibians.*

conditions

noun

All the details of a situation are its **conditions**.

*Some people want better working **conditions**.*

conduct

verb

An object **conducts** sound, heat, or electricity if it lets any of them pass through it.

*Copper wire is used to **conduct** electricity.*

conflict

noun

A **conflict** is a disagreement between people or groups.

*They had a **conflict** about responsibilities at home.*

consumer

noun

A **consumer** eats plants or animals. All animals are consumers.

*A horse is a **consumer** of grass.*

cooperate

verb

When you **cooperate**, you work together.

*We **cooperated** to clean up our messy room.*

country

noun

A **country** is an area that has its own laws and government.

*People can travel from one **country** to another.*

culture

noun

Culture is the way a group of people live: their ideas, their customs, and their traditions.

*It's part of their **culture** to celebrate Cinco de Mayo.*

current

noun

The **current** is the movement of electricity through a wire.

*If the electric **current** does not reach my TV, I can't turn it on.*

custom

noun

A **custom** is a tradition in a culture or a society.

*It is their **custom** to go see the parade on the 4th of July.*

decrease

verb

To **decrease** means to become less or smaller.

*When I spend money, my savings **decrease**.*

demands

noun

Demands are things people ask for strongly.

*Respect for one and all are her **demands**.*

a
b
c
d
e
f
g
h
i
j
k
l
m
n
o
p
q
r
s
t
u
v
w
x
y
z

demonstrate
verb

When you **demonstrate** something, you show or express your feelings or knowledge about it.

*He **demonstrates** his science fair project to the judges.*

distinguish
verb

Distinguish means to tell the difference between two things.

*It's hard to **distinguish** Chris from his twin, Joe.*

diversity
noun

The **diversity** of a group is how different the members of the group are.

*There is a **diversity** of students in my class.*

E

education
noun

An **education** is all the knowledge and skills someone has learned.

*She is proud of her college **education**.*

electrical
adjective

Electrical power comes from an electricity source, such as a wall outlet or a battery.

*The toaster will not work if it's not plugged into an **electrical** outlet.*

emancipation
noun

Emancipation is the act of setting a group of people free.

*After their **emancipation**, many enslaved people started new lives.*

employment
noun

Employment is work someone does to earn money.

*His **employment** brings in extra money.*

energy
noun

Energy is the power to do work.

*It takes a lot of **energy** to run a marathon.*

equality
noun

When people have **equality**, they all have the same rights.

Equality in sports makes it possible for both men and women to play.

escape
verb

To **escape** means to get away from a bad situation.

This dog escapes from his bath!

essential
adjective

Essential means important or necessary.

Water is essential for our survival.

ethnic
adjective

An **ethnic** group is people who share the same culture or race, or are from the same country.

The United States is made up of many ethnic groups.

event
noun

An **event** is something that happens.

The street fair is a big event.

explanation
noun

An **explanation** gives a reason or makes something easy to understand.

The teacher's explanation of DNA was helpful.

food chain
noun

A **food chain** is a sequence of plants and animals in which each feeds on the one below it.

Cats and mice are part of a food chain.

foreign
adjective

If something is **foreign** to you, it is something you have not seen before or is from another country.

You can identify some foreign money by the images on it.

a b c d e f g h i j k l m n o p q r s t u v w x y z

a
b
c
d
e
f
g
h
i
j
k
l
m
n
o
p
q
r
s
t
u
v
w
x
y
z

freedom
noun

Freedom is being able to say, think, and do what you want.

*A bird has the **freedom** to fly.*

heat
noun

Heat is warmth from something that is hot.

*Our cat likes the **heat** from the fireplace.*

herbivore
noun

A **herbivore** is an animal that only eats plants.

*A rabbit is a **herbivore**.*

identity
noun

Your **identity** makes you who you are.

*Playing music is part of this boy's **identity**.*

immigration
noun

Immigration is when you come to live in a country that is not where you were born.

*The early 1900s was a time of great **immigration** from Europe to the U.S.*

insulate
verb

To **insulate** something is to wrap or cover it so that heat, cold, or electricity will not get in or out.

*If you **insulate** your pipes, they won't freeze when it gets cold.*

investigate
verb

When you **investigate** something, you try to find out more about it.

*She **investigates** the insects on the leaf.*

labor
noun

Labor is the hard work someone does.

*A lot of time and **labor** goes into making a chair.*

law
noun

A **law** is a government's official rule.

*The police remind people to follow the **law**.*

M

magnify

verb

When you **magnify** something, you make it appear larger.

*The butterfly wings are easier to see when you **magnify** them.*

microscope

noun

A **microscope** is something that lets you see very small things by magnifying them, or making them look larger.

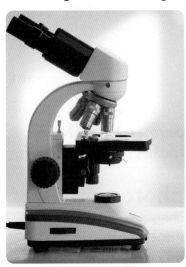

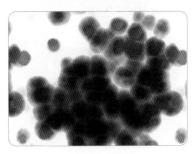

*You can see red blood cells with a **microscope**.*

N

nonviolence

noun

Nonviolence is to not use force.

*These people believe in **nonviolence**. Their protest is peaceful.*

nutrients

noun

Nutrients are things found in food that help plants, animals, and people survive.

*The **nutrients** in fruit and vegetables help people stay healthy.*

O

observe

verb

Observe means to watch someone or something closely.

*He **observes** birds in the trees.*

obstacle

noun

An **obstacle** is something that stops you from succeeding.

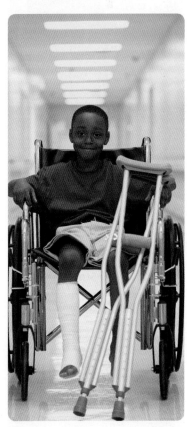

*A broken leg is an **obstacle** to riding a bike.*

a b c d e f g h i j k l **m** **n** **o** p q r s t u v w x y z a b c d e f g h i j k l m n **o** **p** q r s t u v w x y z

omnivore

noun

An **omnivore** is an animal that eats both plants and other animals.

*Bears are **omnivores**.*

opportunity

noun

An **opportunity** is a good chance to do something.

*There is a job **opportunity** here.*

oppose

verb

Oppose means to disagree with an idea or action.

*They protested to **oppose** the government's decision.*

origin

noun

An **origin** is the beginning of something or where something came from.

*The **origin** of chocolate is the cacao bean.*

partnership

noun

Individuals in a **partnership** work together and share the results of their work.

*The kids formed a **partnership** to sell cookies and lemonade.*

photosynthesis

noun

Photosynthesis is the process that plants use to make their food.

*A scientist grows plants to study **photosynthesis**.*

plantation
noun

A **plantation** is a large farm, usually in a hot place, which grows crops such as coffee, cotton, or sugar.

*This tea **plantation** is in Japan.*

power
noun

Power is strength or energy.

*This machine has the **power** to lift heavy things.*

producer
noun

A **producer** makes its own food and produces food energy for other living things, too.

*This bush is a **producer** of blueberries.*

propose
verb

Propose means to suggest something, such as an idea or plan.

*He **proposes** that his mom buy the blue shirt.*

protest
verb

When you **protest**, you show that you do not like or agree with something.

*The teacher **protests** the late submission of the paper.*

reflect
verb

When light hits a mirror, it **reflects** the image, so you can see it.

*When a mirror **reflects** an image, the image is reversed.*

refuge
noun

A **refuge** is a place where people go to be safe or to find shelter.

*These people found **refuge** from the rain.*

rely
verb

If you **rely** on something, you need it.

*We **rely** on electricity in our home.*

a b c d e f g h i j k l m n o **p** q **r** s t u v w x y z

a b c d e f g h i j k l m n o p q **r** **s** t u v w x y z

require

verb

Require means to need.

*A plant **requires** sunlight to survive.*

risk

verb

When you **risk** something, you are in danger of losing or harming it.

*If she does not wear a helmet, she **risks** hurting herself.*

route

noun

A **route** is a path to get from one place to another.

*Use a map to find a **route** to the ocean.*

S

slavery

noun

Slavery is when one person owns another person.

***Slavery** was abolished in the United States by an amendment to the Constitution.*

society

noun

A **society** is a group of people who share rules and customs.

*Our **society** has safety rules.*

solar

adjective

Solar is something that comes from the sun.

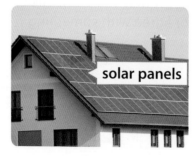

solar panels

***Solar** power heats and cools this home.*

specialize

verb

To **specialize** is to learn or know a lot about one thing.

*He **specializes** in fixing bicycles.*

store

verb

When you **store** something, you keep it somewhere until it is needed.

*They **store** their stuffed bunny with the towels.*

strike

noun

A **strike** is when people don't work because they do not agree with the boss or the company they work for.

*These people are on **strike**.*

symbol

noun

A **symbol** is something that stands for something else.

*A heart shape is a **symbol** for love.*

theory

noun

A **theory** is an idea that explains something.

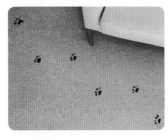

*Her **theory** is that the dog did it.*

thermal

adjective

Something is called **thermal** when it is hot.

*The water sprays out of this geyser because of the **thermal** energy in Earth. The water is very hot!*

transfer

verb

Transfer means to move from one place to another.

*She **transfers** the food to the plate.*

transition

noun

A **transition** is a change from one situation to another.

*Moving to a new city is a big **transition**.*

translate

verb

When you **translate**, you change words and ideas from one language to another.

*Do you speak sign language, or do you need someone to **translate** for you?*

transmit

verb

To **transmit** something means to move it from one place or person to another.

a b c d e f g h i j k l m n o p q r **s** **t** u v w x y z

transmit (continued)

*When we use the phone, my voice **transmits** to my friend's ear.*

volt

noun

Volts are used to measure the force of electrical currents, and the amount of power stored in a battery.

*This battery stores nine **volts** of power.*

watt

noun

A **watt** is a unit for measuring electrical power.

*A light bulb with more **watts** has more power, so it shines brighter.*

Index

Index of Authors

Index of Illustrators

Text and Illustrator Credits

Unit One

Penguin Group (USA) Inc.: Excerpt(s) and illustrations from *I Was Dreaming to Come to America: Memories from the Ellis Island Oral History Project* selected and illustrated by Veronica Lawlor, copyright © 1995 by Veronica Lawlor. Used by permission of Viking Children's Books, an imprint of Penguin Young Readers Group, a division of Penguin Random House LLC. All rights reserved.

Unit Two

Andrea Brown Literary Agency, Inc: Excerpt from *Ten Suns: A Chinese Legend* by Eric A. Kimmel. Copyright © 1998 by Eric A. Kimmel. Reprinted by permission of Andrea Brown Literary Agency, Inc. Illustrations by Marilee Heyer.

Unit Three

Boyd Mills Press: Excerpt from *Coyote and Badger: Desert Hunters of the Southwest* by Bruce Hiscock. Text and photographs copyright © 2001 by Bruce Hiscock. Published by Caroline House, an imprint of Boyd Mills Press, Inc. Reprinted with the permission of the author.

Tilbury House Publishers: "Phyto-power!" from *Sea Soup: Phytoplankton* by Mary M. Cerullo. Copyright © 1999 by Mary M. Cerullo. Reprinted by permission of Tilbury House, Publishers.

Unit Four

Cinco Puntos Press: Excerpt from *Crossing Bok Chitto* by Tim Tingle. Copyright © 2006 by Tim Tingle. Reprinted by permission of Cinco Puntos Press. www.cincopuntos.com. All rights reserved.

Photographic Credits

Cover Humza Deas. iii (tl) rkl_foto/Shutterstock.com (tr) picture alliance/Getty Images (bl) MediaProduction/Getty Images (br) Steve Debenport/Getty Images. 2–3 rkl_foto/Shutterstock.com. 5 (t) Tom Bible/Alamy Stock Photo (tr) Eric Fowke/PhotoEdit (br) Exactostock-1557/Superstock (tl) Volina/Shutterstock.com (bl) iStock.com/alejandrophotography. 7 (tl) Lars Klove/The Image Bank/Getty Images (tc) Photo Central/Alamy Stock Photo (tr) ckaeseberg/Shutterstock.com (bl) Purestock/Alamy Stock Photo (bc) Robin Sachs/PhotoEdit. 30 LL/Roger Viollet/Getty Images. 39 (tl) oliale72/E+/Getty Images (r) Jeff Greenberg/Alamy Stock Photo (bl) Markus Mainka/Shutterstock.com (bc) Nir Darom/Shutterstock.com (br) Quang Ho/Shutterstock.com. 41 (tl) robertharding/Alamy Stock photo (tc) Relaximages/Alamy Stock Photo (tr) Yellow Dog Productions/DigitalVision/Getty Images (bl) Thomas Northcut/Getty Images (bc) DAVID MUSCROFT/Alamy Stock Photo. 42 EVERETT COLLECTION, INC. 44–45 Bill Bachmann/Alamy Stock Photo. 46 Colin McPherson/Getty Images. 47 Bill Bachmann/Alamy Stock Photo. 48 TAO Images Limited/Alamy Stock Photo. 50 (inset) Pawel Libera/Getty Images (bkgd) Luca Pescucci/Alamy Stock Photo. 51 Minerva Studio/Shutterstock.com. 52 Keith Brofsky/Getty Images. 53 Dave Robertson/Alamy Stock Photo. 54 vwalakte/Getty Images. 55 Betsie Van Der Meer/Getty Images. 56 (l) GaudiLab/Shutterstock.com (r) James Baigrie/Getty Images. 57 (t) Thomas Barwick/Getty Images (b) SHAUN CURRY/Getty Images. 58 (bkgd) IakovKalinin/iStock/Getty Images (br) Mohammed Anwarul Kabir Choudhury/Alamy Stock Photo. 59 (b) Vadim Petrakov/Shutterstock.com (inset) ZUMA Press, Inc./Alamy Stock Photo. 60 DAMIEN MEYER/Getty Images. 63 (tl) Brian Bailey/Getty Images (tcl) Rafael Elias/Getty Images (tcr) i_am_zews/Shutterstock.

com (tr) Westend61/Getty Images. 64 Brian Bailey/Getty Images. 65 Rafael Elias/Getty Images. 66 i_am_zews/Shutterstock. 67 Westend61/Getty Images. 70 (l) Martin Lee/Alamy Stock Photo (r) China Span LLC/Danita Delimont Stock Photography. 73 China Span LLC/Danita Delimont Stock Photography. 74 (t) rkl_foto/Shutterstock.com (br) Photosindia Collection/photosindia/Getty Images. 75 (tl) Susan Law Cain/Shutterstock.com (bl) vrenKalinbacak/Shutterstock.com (br) indykb/Shutterstock.com (tc) Knorre/Shutterstock.com(tr) Regisser/Shutterstock.com. 76–77 picture alliance/Getty Images. 78 drewhadley/Getty Images. 81 (tl) STOCK4B/Getty Images (tc) Don Tran/Shutterstock.com (tr) BananaStock/Getty Images (bl) bogdanhoda/Shutterstock.com (bc) Radius Images/Alamy Stock Photo. 99 Eric Kimmel. 102 Albachiaraa/Shutterstock.com. 104 Anan Kaewkhammul/Shutterstock.com. 112 aaaaimages/Getty Images. 115 (tl) neal and molly jansen/Alamy Stock Photo (tc) White Packert/The Image Bank/Getty Images (tr) rixxo/Shutterstock.com (bc) laughingmango/E+/Getty Images (bl) ER Productions Limited/Getty Images. 118–119 Michael Melford/National Geographic Image Collection. 120 Thomas Culhane/National Geographic Image Collection. 121 Thomas Culhane/National Geographic Image Collection. 123 (tl) Serg64/Shutterstock.com (b) Tatiana Popova/Shutterstock.com. 124 acilo/Getty Images. 126 (tr) Thomas Culhane/National Geographic Image Collection (bl) Thomas Culhane/National Geographic Image Collection. 131 (t) Thomas Culhane/National Geographic Image Collection (c) Thomas Culhane/National Geographic Image Collection (b) Thomas Culhane/National Geographic Image Collection. 132 (t) Thomas Culhane/National Geographic Image Collection (bl) Thomas Culhane/National Geographic Image Collection. 133 (t) Thomas Culhane/National Geographic Image Collection (c) Thomas Culhane/National Geographic Image Collection (r) Thomas Culhane/National Geographic Image Collection. 134 Thomas Culhane/National Geographic Image Collection. 136 Albachiaraa/Shutterstock.com. 137 (l) John Mead/Science Source (r) Mark Thiessen/Hampton-Brown/National Geographic Image Collection. 138 Mark Thiessen/Hampton-Brown/National Geographic Image Collection. 139 (tl) Mark Thiessen/Hampton-Brown/National Geographic Image Collection (tr) Mark Thiessen/Hampton-Brown/National Geographic Image Collection (bl) Mark Thiessen/Hampton-Brown/National Geographic Image Collection (bc) Mark Thiessen/Hampton-Brown/National Geographic Image Collection. 140 (tl) Mark Thiessen/Hampton-Brown/National Geographic Image Collection (tr) Mark Thiessen/Hampton-Brown/National Geographic Image Collection (bl) Mark Thiessen/Hampton-Brown/National Geographic Image Collection (br) Mark Thiessen/Hampton-Brown/National Geographic Image Collection. 141 (tl) Mark Thiessen/Hampton-Brown/National Geographic Image Collection (tr) Mark Thiessen/Hampton-Brown/National Geographic Image Collection (bl) Mark Thiessen/Hampton-Brown/National Geographic Image Collection. 148 picture alliance/Getty Images. 149 Pavel K/Shutterstock.com. 150–151 MediaProduction/Getty Images. 153 (t) Kevin Schafer/Getty Images (tc) BirdImages/iStock/Getty Images (bc) FloridaStock/Shutterstock.com (b) Arthur Tilley/Getty Images. 155 (tl) Oote Boe 3/Alamy Stock Photo (tc) Elena Elisseeva/Shutterstock.com (tr) Richard Hutchings/PhotoEdit (bl) Summer Jones/Alamy Stock Photo (bc) Michael Newman/PhotoEdit. 157 Hannamariah/Shutterstock.com. 172 (l) NORBERT ROSING/National Geographic Image Collection (r) Konrad Wothe/Minden Pictures. 173 (l) Bruce Hiscock (tr) Bruce Hiscock. 177 (bkgd) JeniFoto/Shutterstock.com (bl) Bill Florence/Shutterstock.com (b) Merlin D. Tuttle/Getty Images (br) Tom Vezo/Minden Pictures/Superstock. 178–179 NORBERT ROSING/

National Geographic Image Collection. 179 (tr) George Grall/National Geographic/Getty Images (c) Viktor Loki/Shutterstock.com (b) Jo Ann Snover/Shutterstock.com. 180 Thomas Hallstein/Alamy Stock Photo. 183 (t) Daniel Hebert/Shutterstock.com (b) Siede Preis/Getty Images. 187 (tl) brackish_nz/Shutterstock.com (tl) GK Hart/Vikki Hart/Getty Images (tc) Glowimages/Getty Images (tr) Blacqbook/Shutterstock.com (bl) Jose Luis Pelaez Inc/Getty Images (bc) Cindy Charles/PhotoEdit. 189 Jose Manuel Gelpi Diaz/Dreamstime. 191 Mike Johnson Marine Natural History Photography. 192 Mike Johnson Marine Natural History Photography. 193 Courtesy of Tierney Thys. 195 (t) Watt Jim/Getty Images. 194–95 Istock.com/DJMattaar. 196 Ilukee/Alamy Stock Photo. 197 Mike Johnson Marine Natural History Photography. 198–199 Stephen Frink/Getty Images. 199 (tr) Robert Sisson/National Geographic Image Collection (bl) Willard Culver/National Geographic Image Collection (bc) NathanChor/Getty Images. 201 Odua Images/Shutterstock.com. 202 Mike Johnson Marine Natural History Photography. 204 (bl) Danita Delimont/Alamy Stock Photo (c) Tomas Kotouc/Shutterstock.com. 205 (bkgd) Reinhard Dirscherl/Alamy Stock Photo (bl) Facanv/Shutterstock.com (tr) Visual&Written SL/Alamy (br) Paul Zahl/National Geographic/Getty Images. 206 feathercollector/Shutterstock.com. 208 Tomas Kotouc/Shutterstock. 209 Emory Kristof/National Geographic/Getty Images. 201 (tr) Steve Gschmeissner/Science Source (br) Steve Gschmeissner/Science Source (bl) Steve Gschmeissner/Science Source. 213 twphotos/E+/Getty Images. 215 Jupiterimages/Getty Images. 219 Design Pics Inc/Alamy Stock Photo. 220 (t) MediaProduction/Getty Images (tr) Stephen Frink/DigitalVision/Getty Images (tcr) Arco Peter/Getty Images (cr) Jupiterimages/Getty Images (bcr) Roland Birke/Photolibrary/Getty Images (br) Scenics & Science/Alamy Stock Photo. 221 (l) Stephen Frink/DigitalVision/Getty Images (br) Michael Newman/PhotoEdit. 222–223 Steve Debenport/Getty Images. 224 Everett Historical/Shutterstock.com. 227 (tl) Kris Timken/Blend Images/Getty Images(tcl) Jason Lee/REUTERS (tcr) Rick Scuteri/REUTERS (tr) PhotoAlto/Laurence Mouton/Getty Images (bl) David Young-Wolff/PhotoEdit (bc) meshaphoto/Getty Images. 229 Jim Arbogast/Getty Images. 248 (tl) Annmarie Young/Shutterstock (tcl) Harold R. Stinnette Photo Stock/Alamy Stock Photo (tcr) hrstovcnet/Deposit Photos (tr) Lisovskaya Natalia/Shutterstock.com. 249 Library of Congress, Prints & Photographs Division, Reproduction number LC-DIG-cwpb-00218 (digital file from original neg.) LC-B8171-518 (b&w film neg.). 250 (bkgd) MPI/Archive Photos/Getty Images (bl) Lagui/Shutterstock (inset) Ohio History Connection. 251 Rose Zgodzinski. 252 Courtesy of the Ohio History Connection. 253 Courtesy of the Ohio History Connection. 257 (tl) Bettmann/Getty Images (bl) Marmaduke St. John/Alamy Stock Photo (r) Thomas Lohnes/Getty Images. 259 (tl) Peter Turnley/Getty Images (tc) maximino/Shutterstock (tr) Tony Freeman/PhotoEdit (bl) Mark Richard/PhotoEdit (bc) Maryunin Yury Vasilevich/Shutterstock.com. 262–263 Anita van Zyl/Gallo Images/Getty Images. 264 WALTER DHLADHLA/Getty Images. 265 Hein Von Horstein/Getty Images 266 WHA/World History Archive/akg-images. 267 AFP/Getty Images. 268 History and Art Collection/Alamy. 269 Terence Spencer/Getty Images. 270 Gallo Images/Getty Images. 271 akg-images/Africa Media Online. 272 Africa Media Online/akg-images. 273 Times Media/akg-images. 274 Africa Media Online/akg-images. 275 David Turnley/Getty Images. 276 Trinity Mirror / Mirrorpix/Alamy Stock Photo. 277 Chip Somodevilla/Getty Images. 278 Anita van Zyl/Gallo Images/Getty Images. 280 Lisa F. Young/Dreamstime.com. 281 Laurent Weyl/Panos Pictures/Redux. 282 (t) Koldunov/Getty Images (inset) Rich Carey/Shutterstock.com. 283 (t)

Acknowledgments

The Authors and Publisher would like to thank the following reviewers and teaching professionals for their valuable feedback during the development of the series.

Literature Reviewers

Carmen Agra Deedy, Grace Lin, Jonda C. McNair, Anastasia Suen

Global Reviewers

USA/Canada:

Terrie Armstrong, Bilingual/ESL Program Team Leader, Houston Independent School District, Houston, TX; **Julie Folkert,** Language Arts Coordinator, Farmington Public Schools, Farmington, MI; **Norma Godina-Silva, Ph.D,** Bilingual Education/ESL/Title III Consultant, ESL-BilingualResources.com, El Paso, TX; **Keely Krueger,** Director of Bilingual Education, Woodstock Community Unit School 200, Woodstock, IL; **Myra Junyk,** Literacy Consultant, Toronto, ON; **Irma Bravo Lawrence,** Director II, District and English Learner Support Services, Stanislaus County Office of Education, Turlock, CA; **Lore Levene,** Coordinator of Language Arts, NBCT Community Consolidated School District 59, Mt. Prospect, IL; **Estee Lopez,** Professor of Literacy Education and ELL Specialist, College of New Rochelle, New Rochelle, NY; **Christine Kay Williams,** ESOL Teacher, Baltimore County Public Schools, Baltimore, MD

Asia:

Mohan Aiyer, School Principal, Brainworks International School, Yangon; **Andrew Chuang,** Weige Primary School, Taipei; **Sherefa Dickson,** Head Teacher, SMIC, Beijing; **Ms Hien,** IP Manager, IPS Vietnam, Ho Chi Minh; **Christine Huang,** Principal, The International Bilingual School at the Hsinchu Science Park (IBSH), Hsinchu; **Julie Hwang,** Academic Consultant, Seoul; **David Kwok,** CEO, Englit Enterprise, Guangzhou; **Emily Li,** Teaching Assistant, SMIC, Beijing; **Warren Martin,** English Teacher, Houhai English, Beijing; **Bongse Memba,** Academic Coordinator, SMIC, Beijing; **Hoai Minh Nguyen,** Wellspring International Bilingual School, Ho Chi Minh; **Mark Robertson,** Elementary School Principal, Yangon Academy, Yangon; **Daphne Tseng,** American Eagle Institute, Hsinchu; **Amanda Xu,** Director of Teaching and Research, Englit Enterprise, Guangzhou; **Alice Yamamoto,** ALT, PL Gakuen Elementary School, Osaka; **Yan Yang,** Director of Research Development, Houhai English, Beijing

Middle East:

Lisa Olsen, Teacher, GEMS World Academy, Dubai, United Arab Emirates; **Erin Witthoft,** Curriculum Coordinator, Universal American School, Kuwait

Latin America:

Federico Brull, Academic Director, Cambridge School of Monterrey, Mexico; **Elizabeth Caballero,** English Coordinator, Ramiro Kolbe Campus Otay, Mexico; **Renata Callipo,** Teacher, CEI Romualdo, Brazil; **Lilia Huerta,** General Supervisor, Ramiro Kolbe Campus Presidentes, Mexico; **Rosalba Millán,** English Coordinator Primary, Instituto Cenca, Mexico; **Ann Marie Moreira,** Academic Consultant, Brazil; **Raúl Rivera,** English Coordinator, Ramiro Kolbe Campus Santa Fe, Mexico; **Leonardo Xavier,** Teacher, CEI Romualdo, Brazil

The Publisher gratefully acknowledges the contributions of the following National Geographic Explorers to our program and planet:

Thomas Culhane and Tierny Thys